# Where the
# Love
# Is

Other books by GORDON R. MCLEAN

*We're Holding Your Son*
*High on the Campus*
    Haskell Bowen, co-author
*How to Raise Your Parents and*
    *Other Helpful Advice for Teens*

# Where the Love Is

## Gordon R. McLean

WORD BOOKS, Publisher
Waco, Texas

To
JIM BUCHFUEHRER and RAY RAMSEY
who have learned with me that
people may go where the action is
but they'll stay
where the love is

# Contents

# Foreword

Man is made for love. His highest joy in life is in loving and being loved. There is nothing stronger or more pleasant, and the greatest delight that can be enjoyed is knowing God's love right here, right now. God bears a tender affection for us and reveals that love in so many ways, but the supreme expression of his love is the Lord Jesus Christ. "For God loved the world so much that he gave his only Son so that anyone who believes in him shall not perish, but have eternal life" (John 3:16, LB). He asks that we respond to that love by a firm, unconditional, and eternal commitment to Jesus Christ that transforms our lives, making us "Christ's ones," or Christians.

The Christian then expresses love for his fellow-men when he accepts them as they are with their sins and their failures and offers no hindrance to the free flow of God's love toward them. This is the hardest lesson in Christianity to learn. To love people even in their sin is a likeness of God's love which we are to practice without talking about it—without thought of return.

Gordon McLean has learned that love is the light that breaks through prison doors, and, in a thousand different ways, his unselfish expression of love for people has resulted in their having experienced the ultimate in God's love . . . salvation from the penalty and power of sin.

*Where the Love Is* tells us that love is an overworked word for an unemployed emotion that exists, not in gazing starry-eyed into the face of God but in looking forward and moving in the same direction with him.

BILLY ZEOLI
President
Gospel Films, Inc.

# Preface

In many ways this book is a diary, my own adventures in the Christian faith. Thus it is a very personal book, and for that I make no apologies. My life has not always been easy, but I have much to be thankful for and much to live for. It is this excitement I am anxious to share with you on these pages. But more than my experiences, I hope our Lord is seen here as he has worked in my life and in my friends whom you will read about.

I have been fortunate to have been able to work closely with some of the outstanding Christian leaders of our day; these people have had a profound effect upon my life and ministry. Others through their writings have provided valuable guidance and inspiration. The thoughts and guidance of these men are on these pages; I make no claim at originating the insights of this material.

My grateful thanks goes to those who helped in the preparation of this book: my secretary, Anne Claussen, who typed the manuscript; Clyde Vandeburg of Vandeburg-Linkletter Associates, my agent; Richard Bothman and the Santa Clara County Juvenile Probation Department; the staff at KLIV radio; and my associates in Youth for Christ/Campus Life. Some of this material originally appeared as articles by me in *Guideposts*, *Campus Life*, and *Power* and is reprinted here by permission.

GORDON McLEAN

# Introduction

This is a book about life—the rich, full, and satisfying life a person can know when Jesus Christ is at the center of his living. And that is something I can understand very well.

I'm a college student, but it was during my junior year in high school that I learned how meaningful knowing the Lord can really be. Perhaps I was a little more ready than most people to listen; I was in a terrible jam and I needed help, but at the time I didn't suspect God would have anything to do with it, or me.

As a freshman in high school, I got into the drug scene. A little curiosity and a desire to be one of the boys was all it took to get me started. It was easy to convince myself that a little grass (marijuana) never hurt anybody, even though my grades, sports, and activities quickly went down the tubes. My next lie was that I would never use anything but grass, but that ended when I went on to acid (L.S.D.), reds (seconal), and speed (methedrine). Drug involvement can be expensive, and one of the simplest ways to finance the use can be by furnishing drugs to other students. I was soon in business with a friend, and a profitable one, too, dealing between three hundred and six hundred dollars a week at my school and in my neighborhood. It's not the sinister adult figure in black hanging around campus who does most of the selling. If you want to stop drug pushers to teens, you're going to have to reach students like me; students deal with each other.

The more we sold, the more loose (careless) we got. One day I sold two kilos of grass to a man who later turned out to be an undercover agent for the Santa Clara County, California, narcotics bureau. I was soon busted and taken to juvenile hall.

I wasn't a stranger to the place. I can remember sitting in juvenile hall, scared and wondering what would happen next. Everything I had based my security on— the drugs, the crowd, the girls—was gone, and I was well on my way to an institution.

My probation officer introduced me to Gordon McLean, a man who has done a lot of counseling work with kids in my situation. He'll tell you about talking with me later on in these pages. We got well acquainted, and he talked about something that could make a difference in my whole way of living, a personal relationship with Jesus Christ. I really didn't think I needed anything a preacher might offer; sixteen years of religion had not done much for me. But there was something very real sounding and compelling about what Gordon was saying.

One afternoon in the chaplain's office at the hall I accepted Christ. I wasn't really sure of what I had done or where it would lead me, but I do know something happened in that office when I prayed. I haven't been the same since! I've made my mistakes and fought some real battles within myself and with my old crowd, but it's been a wonderful new life. I'm getting stronger every day and am learning new things about this Christian faith that are really exciting.

The court gave me a good break and let me go home on probation. You might well argue that was too lenient a disposition of my case, and you may well be right. But the probation officer and the judge believed me when I said I had changed and was not going back to drugs. I haven't.

I've worked with Mr. McLean, speaking to adult and student audiences all over the country. I had the wonderful opportunity to spend several weeks in Brazil sharing my experiences with students in São Paulo and later reporting on that trip on national television in this country with Art Linkletter. Mr. McLean has told my story in his book *High on the Campus*, and I was one of the teenagers who appeared in the motion picture adaptation of the book. Since then I've taught a class of high-school students in my church, worked in a Campus Life Club, done some speaking, and helped produce Gordon's radio show, "Speak Out," on KLIV in San Jose. I want to devote my life to working with other young people, perhaps as a probation officer. In the process, my faith in Christ has become much stronger, and my joy in serving him is very real.

You'll have to agree all this represents quite a change for a guy who was a teenage pusher.

And that's what this book is all about. The changes Christ can make in the lives of people, not just a young person on drugs. Jesus Christ is where it's at . . . what's happening right now . . . where the love is.

FRANK C. ROBERTS

# Chapter 1

# *Big Deal*

A FORMER GENERATION set out to prove whether there was or was not a God.

Today's generation asks, "What difference does it make?"

Plenty.

But a skeptical generation says, "Don't bother me with that God stuff. I'm concerned about war, poverty, racial hatred, pollution, crime . . . the big issues. Let's do something about those things. That's where the action is!"

And, of course, the action is there. Only one thing— the problems are still a long way from being solved. In some cases, we're not even finding a route to the solution.

Let me suggest one reason why these issues are not being solved. Because we treat them as problems and they aren't!

"What? You mean to say that war, environment, and prejudice aren't our problems?"

That's right. They are *symptoms* of some very basic

underlying problems that much of our society hasn't begun to recognize, let alone deal with.

My premise is simply: the problem is not what man *does*, it is what man *is*. What a man is will determine what he does.

Here's what Thomas Harris says about our sick society: "Slums and ghettos and put-downs are not going to disappear in society unless slums and games disappear from the hearts of people. . . . What society *should* do is one thing. What individuals *dare* do is another." [1]

The Bible says the basic problem lies in the nature of man. "The heart is the most deceitful thing there is, and desperately wicked. No one can really know how bad it is!" (Jer. 17:9, LB).

And Dr. Thomas Harris agrees. "Sin, or badness, or evil, or 'human nature,' whatever we call the flaw in our species, is apparent in every person. We simply cannot argue with the endemic 'cussedness' of man. . . . The harder he fights, the greater his sin, the more skillful become his games, the more ulterior becomes his life, until he does, in fact, feel the great estrangement, or separateness . . . sin." [2]

*If* we could change man, then we could change our society and world. But that's a big *if*.

Is transforming men an impossible dream?

No!

Because God, in the twentieth-century computerized space age, is still changing men who come to know him.

So often a cynic will ask, "If there's a God up there,

---

1. Thomas Harris, *I'm OK—You're OK* (New York: Harper & Row, 1969), p. 229.
2. Ibid., p. 225.

why doesn't he do something about all the mess around us?" He has. Two thousand years ago he visited this earth. When he arrived, only two kinds of people found him at the stable—simple shepherds and wise men. And those wise men were convinced they didn't know everything and were willing to look beyond the limits of their intellect, culture, and experience.

Moreover, he "laid it on the line" by dying. And three days later he came back to life to prove that everything he offered, claimed, and taught was true. Significantly, a loyal group of his followers, once skeptics themselves, were willing to give their lives for their belief in him and his resurrection. In the process they turned the world upside down.

It didn't all stop two thousand years ago. It's still happening.

God's love is a present fact; we can *know* it. We can also *experience* it, and in these pages you'll meet people from all walks of life who have done exactly that.

Ray, a teenager deeply involved with drugs, split from home when he and his quarreling family had all they could stand of each other. He tried making it on his own, but lost his job, turned to drugs, and finally on a wild acid trip at a rock festival attacked some police officers.

Ray went to the hospital, then to jail, and finally to the James Ranch, the Santa Clara County juvenile rehabilitation facility. He had many problems, but most of all he felt alone, rejected, and bitter. Ray was looking desperately for love.

One evening in the dining hall I opened my pocket Testament and showed him one of the most familiar verses in the whole Bible, John 3:16. I could see the words almost leap from the page to the eyes and then to the mind of this lonely young fellow.

"Hey, man, is that for real?" he asked.

"It sure is. And if you'll respond to what that says, Ray, you can experience the greatest love a man can ever know, right here, right now!"

And Ray did. He quietly prayed with me, and in that very unemotional setting something happened in that boy's life that had him smiling and happy for the first time in many months.

Now, several years later, Ray is still growing in the faith that he turned loose in his life that night. He's a college student, youth group leader, counselor, and his family is together now like they've never been before. Things like that happen when you experience love.

Then, you can *learn* to love. A tool isn't much use if you don't know how to use it. Love is good only if you learn to let it control your life.

What is the Christian measure of love? You know it. It's the very familiar phrase that came from the lips of our Lord, "Love your neighbor as yourself."

That's where the learning comes in. Learning first to love ourselves and then other people.

To begin, we must get to know ourselves. Let's start by admitting we're not always the completely-in-control, mature person we like people to think we are.

In our transactions with other people, we often react on the level of feeling. And the result of the frustrating, civilizing process of growing up is most often negative feelings, producing an "I'm not OK, you're OK" reaction.

Even after childhood years, we can often find ourselves retreating to this emotional and inadequate level of response aptly called by Dr. Thomas Harris acting out our *child*.

But there's a counterforce at work within us replaying the taught concepts of life, often well impressed as a pattern of values in the first five years of life. Our internal *parent* is at work feeding standards, prejudices, and often guilt reactions. Trying to come out on top is our *adult*, that part of us that wants to be free from the stereotyped responses of the parent and the emotional pitfalls of the child so as to be able to make sensible, logical, free adult choices after carefully considering all the options.

Learning to understand the roles of the child, parent, and adult, the various games played between them, and the correcting of the immaturity needed for full adult control is called *transactional analysis*. It's a comparatively new concept of personality treatment that is a remarkable tool for group, individual, and even personal therapy. (See *I'm OK—You're OK* by Thomas Harris.)

But often instead of really seeing ourselves as we are, we persist in playing games. (See *Games People Play* and *What Do You Say After You've Said Hello*, both by Dr. Eric Berne.) And whether it is false humility, an inflated sense of importance, or martyrdom . . . none of them make us the kind of confident, self-assured people with a love for ourselves that can offer strength to others.

Dr. Harold Nelson of Swedish Covenant Hospital, Chicago, writing in *Eternity* magazine points out three encounters we must have if we are to follow properly our Lord's command to love ourselves:

We must have *self-awareness*, must make an honest evaluation of both our strengths and weaknesses. A starting point is to try to see ourselves as God sees us, and that is through the eyes of a Savior who loved us enough to die for us. It is true he sees our evil past, our self-indulging ego trips, but he goes beyond that to see us as forgiven through Christ's sacrifice.

We must be *self-accepting*. God accepts us, weaknesses and all. His love is not conditional. Not if I change . . . if I quit certain habits, but just as I am. He does not say, as many of us do to husbands, wives, children, "I'll love you as long as you do what I say. But if you don't . . ." After accepting my limitations, I can be a great deal more tolerant of the weaknesses in others. If God accepts us as we are, we should not do any less for ourselves.

We must be *self-giving;* we cannot love ourselves in isolation. Love is returned to us only as it is given away. There are those who would say, "Love and be loved in return." But man isn't really built that way. He cannot give something he hasn't first received. Ideally he should know the love of a mother and father, but even lacking that, he can know God's love and be capable of loving others.

We can know God's love, experience it, mature in it, and share it.

In my experience some of the greatest examples of this concern have been teen to teen, when a young person cared enough to help a friend. It isn't always the easiest thing to do . . .

"Are you out of your mind?" was Bob's angry response to his brother's suggestion. "So you were caught stealing and spent some time in jail. And you may have to go back. Well, tough luck. They didn't catch me, so there's nothing I have to do about it. That's that!"

"No, it's not!" said Rich, age eighteen and older than his brother by about a year. "Stealing is not a matter of whether you get caught or not, or how much the stuff is worth, it's just wrong."

"What hit you? A couple of days in stir and you're talking like a cop!" Bob fired back defensively.

You couldn't blame Bob for being surprised. The two brothers, high-school students in San Jose and often fierce rivals in sports, were no strangers to arguing with each other. Nor was the fact that either of them was in trouble new—Rich had been to a county juvenile rehabilitation center for burglary and Bob had been committed to a state institution for forceful robbery.

A few days earlier both boys had been in a department store. Rich had shoplifted a small ring while Bob had picked up a pair of shoes. Rich had been caught by an alert young clerk and got his first taste of adult jail. He didn't like the experience, but even more important, something he didn't even know he had began to bother him— his conscience.

"I tried telling myself it was only a small item . . . the store was big and wouldn't really miss it . . . they had insurance for losses like that . . . a lot of kids do it every day . . . but it was no use," Rich relates. "I kept coming back to the same conclusion . . . it was wrong. I was hurting my family, and God knows my parents have been through enough with my brother and me. Some of the guys in the jail told me to play it cool, this was no big thing, and I could beat the rap. But, if they knew so much, how come they were locked up?

"Next, I did a really strange thing. I prayed and asked the Lord to forgive me and help me do what was right. Even in that miserable county jail tank I felt a real peace for the first time in years. I was kinda crying and smiling at the same time and one of the older guys asked, 'What happened to you, kid?' I told him I didn't know for sure but I thought I'd just met God. He looked bewildered and said, 'In here? You must be kidding.' He probably thought I was on drugs or something, but I wasn't. I just knew I wasn't going to be back for any other charges, and I wasn't going to steal any more."

When Rich was released, he decided to confront his brother with what had happened and try to get through to him. It wasn't easy.

"So stealing is wrong, is it Rich? Suppose I tell you I'll quit. What do you expect me to do? Pay for the pair of shoes?"

"Yes!"

They argued back and forth and finally Bob said, "All right, I'll mail the money in a plain envelope and tell them what it's for, but I won't sign my name."

"Coward . . ."

"Okay, you win. I get paid next Saturday, and I'll go in and see the store manager and give him back the money. Now will you get off my back?"

"No," replied Rich. "You and I are too much alike. Unless something really changes inside it won't be long until you're back to the old ways. You know I've changed, and I want to tell you why."

Bob listened, grudgingly at first. This sure didn't sound like the old Rich; he had changed. And Bob began to think about what a commitment to the Lord would mean in his own life.

Bob was in church the day his older brother made a public profession of faith. And I learned the full story from Bob a few weeks later when he made his commitment to the Lord and united with the church.

That's love. Caring enough to do what's right even when it isn't easy.

The initial commitment to Christ is only the starting point in building a maturing, ongoing relationship with the Lord. It is unfortunate that so many people do not grow spiritually through a regular pattern of reading God's Word, developing a closer relationship with God through prayer, and becoming active participants with other believers in his work. This can turn the Christian life from a dull routine into a meaningful walk of service with much to share and learn along the way.

Where are things really happening today? With people. Not just in events or headlines. But in the hearts of men.

*People may go where the action is, but they'll stay where the love is.*

Big deal?

It sure is!

# Chapter 2
## *God at Work*

THE YOUNG MEN sitting across the front row of the prison chapel wondered what would happen next.

So did I.

Older, veteran inmates in an institution will take the daily happening with an unperturbed calm characteristic of the overly familiar, undemanding routine they have chosen to accept behind bars. But not the restless young rebels who, like many of their contemporaries on the outside, find any new unsettling experience a challenge. And it was these young prisoners who made up most of my audience.

Nothing resembling a chapel service had been held for these young men in months. Now they were at one and had no idea what to expect.

The service was mine to conduct. Some of the cynical guards assigned to herd the men into place looked at me with sardonic glances which all but asked their question for them, "O.K., mister, do you think you can reach this crowd?" Their looks served to unnerve me a little more; I was already asking myself the same question.

How had I ever gotten into this situation? There was nothing, absolutely nothing, in my background or style of living that gave me anything in common with this Canadian prison audience.

I had come from a hard working, respectable family. My dad's illness during most of my high-school days and his eventual death had kept us from ever being really close during my crucial teenage years. But I had never lacked for anything, had been taught good moral standards, lived in a decent and quiet neighborhood, and had never been any closer to scandal or crime than seeing the headlines in the *Regina Leader-Post*, the *Vancouver Sun*, or the *Victoria Colonist*. I had enjoyed the privilege of meeting and knowing many of the governmental leaders of the day, and this had given me a deeply impressive and personal lesson in citizenship. But other than that, my growing-up years had been very normal.

There was one significant event during my high-school days that had a profound effect on my life. Some friends took me with them to a youth rally on a Friday night at their church. I went because I wanted to do them a favor in response to their rather persistent invitations for me to attend other like events. I was also frankly curious; I couldn't imagine teenagers attending a religious event on a Friday night. Believe me, there were other things to do, so I had to see for myself what it was that meant so much to these young people.

Well, I found out. That night, for the first time, I faced the fact of God loving me so much he invested nothing less than the life of his only Son that I might know, through

27

him, a rich, full life that would last forever. Two young people made a public commitment to the Lord that night, and I was one of them.

For the life of me, I cannot explain how a somewhat confused young man can quietly bow his head and in simple language invite Christ to become the center of his living and come out of that simple experience a completely changed person. The divine chemistry that mixes human inadequacy with the love of Calvary to produce transformation is beyond my comprehension. But it is not beyond my knowing, for I experienced it that night and, incidentally, have seen its effects in thousands of other lives since.

At first, I was not really sure what had happened, but I felt an inner warmth and satisfaction such as I had never before known. I suspect it is this sensation the drug user tries to reproduce chemically. Unfortunately, he must settle for the temporary, the artificial, and the tragic. That night I experienced the permanent, the real, and the beautiful satisfaction only a man at peace with himself and God can know.

It wasn't the easiest thing to explain either. My friends asked what had happened, and I told them, "I became a Christian," which was really about all I knew. Several of them laughed and replied, "That's all right, you'll get over it!" A girl I dated several times asked, "What on earth happened to you?" I told her it wasn't exactly something on earth that had happened to me, it was something far more lasting than that. She suggested I take an aspirin and lie down for awhile, adding the hope I'd be all right again in a few hours.

I wanted to know what had happened . . . what it

meant . . . where I was going . . . and a lot more about this Person who was now an intrinsic, vital part of my life. The Bible had been used to get us acquainted, and it was to this source I went for further enlightenment. It was the right place to go, and it became my constant guide.

I found a small church near my home with a young pastor and his wife who were eager to welcome new people to their fellowship. This provided me with the spiritual nurture I needed. And it was in their services that the first signs of restlessness set in. It wasn't doubt; the spiritual experience that started me on this road might well be open to elaboration, but its validity was never subject to question, even at the most discouraging of times.

What disturbed me was a gap I sensed between the public pronouncement and the personal performance in many of the members. To be sure there were numerous examples of selfless dedication in the group. This was especially true of the young pastor and his wife and a select group within the congregation. But it was equally obvious that to many reality had long since been replaced by routine.

At testimony time, a standard feature of the weekly evangelistic meeting, I heard many of them talk about "the joy of the Lord," but they said it in rather a matter-of-fact manner without any show of joy or enthusiasm. The service was attended almost exclusively by the very dedicated or, I came to suspect, by those who had a broken television set.

We sang such hymns as "Take my silver and my gold, not a mite would I withhold," but the church, serving a prosperous community, was seemingly always in financial trouble. "Sweet hour of prayer" could more truthfully have been sung by these people, "Sweet fifteen minutes of prayer."

The pastor would faithfully exhort his flock to get the message out to the lost and urged us never to underestimate the gospel power to transform lives. We would echo those sentiments in testimonies, in church school contest promotional announcements, but always to each other, *not* to the people who needed to hear it outside.

There was my problem. I came to the conclusion that if what I had as a Christian was really and genuinely true, then nothing in the whole world mattered so much as telling anyone and everyone I could about it. And if it was not true, then it was better to forget the whole business, and the sooner the better. There could be no middle ground.

I came to a second turning point in my life and said another simple prayer that was to have a profound effect on my life. I said, "God, I don't know what you want with my life, what you want me to do, where you want me to go, but whatever it is you want, that's what I want." Believe me, anyone saying that prayer sincerely should expect to be taken up on it.

The orders weren't long in coming. During the last part of my high-school days I was introduced to the ministry of Youth for Christ with its Bible-centered, contemporary, and vital thrust into the very center of a pagan highschool population. My whole life has been spent since then working with that program. I'm the youngest veteran in YFC!

I enjoyed working with teenagers and their parents and their churches. But I was growing increasingly aware of a whole group we were missing, the kids making the headlines for acts of vandalism, theft, and worse. If Christ can really transform lives, what could he do in the lives of those kids? This was the searing question in my mind as I read the same stories in the papers that upset all of us every day. It's the kind of a question that sent David Wilkerson from a small pastorate in rural Pennsylvania to reach the youth gangs in New York or drew converted underworld figure Jim Vaus from a successful career in electronics to Hell's Gate Station and youth work in the same city. They both love desperate kids for Christ's sake.

For me, it took a visit with a teenager my own age in a prison cell where he was awaiting trial for murder. And it was this same question which drove me back to that same prison week after week to talk to the many hundreds of other teenagers confined there. Evidently, this concerned warden decided that a young Christian talking with the inmates might be one of the better influences they would find behind bars.

And then, finally, we decided to hold that first chapel service. This came from the growing awareness that if I was going to talk with all the young men who wanted to see me, I would have to do it in some sort of a group setting. There just wasn't enough time to see them all individually. So the service was born, and almost died before it started.

An inmate organist played some songs on a little-used chapel instrument. I decided not to try any congregational songs so I stood up to speak.

"Guys, I've met many of you during the last few weeks I've been visiting here, and I've appreciated getting to know you. You've probably wondered why I'm here. Some of you have said that I don't belong in this place and that I should go back to my nice home and good neighborhood. I'm here because I found something I was looking for, and I think many of you are looking for the same thing— real love, inner peace, a sense of purpose in life. God cares about you, and so do I."

Just then a young fellow in the front row shot back, "Don't hand me that 'God loves us' jazz. If he loves us so much, why are we here? Why is there so much hate in the world?" His skin was dark black, but his flashing eyes were white.

I got down from the platform and walked over to him. Although I spoke directly to him, the crowd became very still so as to hear the exchange. "You're right. There is a lot of hate in the world. And part of it is why you're here. Some people only know how to hate, so they lie, steal, and kill. God wants to change that. And people go on hating themselves and their neighbors because they either don't know about God's love or won't accept it. Which is it with you?"

"I don't know about it," he replied.

"Do you want to know about it?"

"Well, yeah, I do. But if God cares so much, how come he never told us about it . . . you know, really proved it?"

"He did. God's great advertisement was a cross . . ."

These guys weren't an easy crowd, and they taught me a great deal while I was ministering to them. It was unusual for a preacher to have murderers, dopers, and thieves as his friends, but these fellows were just that. Sure, some of them tried to use me and play their angles, and I wasn't always smart enough to catch on. Let's face it, anytime you want to help people, that's a risk you take. But what is surprising is how many weren't playing a game, wanted help, and were searching for a way out of the entangled web that had become their way of life.

But how can you tell who is sincere and who is playing some form of con game with Christianity as a front?

You can't. That is the risk of being involved with people. If you never allow yourself to be open and available to help people, you will never be hurt or disappointed. Whenever you are open, there is the possibility of being disappointed. I've had it happen. My car has been stolen and wrecked. The home of one of my closest friends was later burglarized by a boy they had taken in as a foster child. I've seen a young person who appeared sincere and showed every promise of making good, but definitely didn't make it. And the only consolation I know of is that I've never met any expert who knew how to unfailingly predict success and failure with other people. There are no magic crystal balls.

But there are the obvious pitfalls to avoid—the signs in attitude and conduct which serve as danger signals, but even here, the results are not infallible. There have been those from time to time who I thought wouldn't make it, and yet they have turned into some of the greatest success stories. I've learned long ago that God is keeping score on the results of faithful Christian witness, not me. My job is to be his faithful servant and witness; the final results are in other hands.

And there are results.

"Why doesn't God get involved?" I'm often asked by questioning students. "If there really is a God, why doesn't he do something to show he's there?" is another frequently asked question.

God is alive, healthy, and doing very well. The tragedy is that so many people simply haven't noticed. They look for intervention in the political scene or some spectacular sign in the sky instead of where God is at work—in the lives of people.

What is the greatest miracle?

A one-night spectacular in the heavens? If that impresses you, go to the Arctic Circle and view the northern lights.

What about divine healing?

"Is there any other kind?" A doctor can set a broken bone, but only God can mend it. And even the most skillful of physicians is said to be practicing medicine—still learning about the wonders of the human body.

Divine intervention in the affairs of men? If that is where you look for evidence of God at work, check out the survival of the little nation of Israel. The newspapers can tell you what is happening there today; the Bible will tell you what will happen there tomorrow!

Now let me pose a question: *Is not the greatest evidence of God's love, concern, and power expressed in the transformation of a human life?* Is there anything greater than taking those trapped in the empty wastelands of twentieth-century materialism and transforming them into people with goals, meaning, and satisfaction to their lives? Psychiatric counseling and therapy aim for this but when attempted without God's guidance, often fall far short. However, people who encounter Christ find those values and are never the same again. The change he makes is so complete that John refers to it in the Bible as a "new birth" and declares men won't see, let alone enter, the

Kingdom of God without it. Paul describes it this way, "When someone becomes a Christian he becomes a brand new person inside. He is not the same any more. A new life has begun!" (2 Cor. 5:17, LB).

It makes little difference who the person is, his background, skin color, or standing in life—Christ meets him where he is, at the point of his greatest need, and brings him to an exciting new plane of living. That is not merely a philosophical theory. It was this I was looking for, evidence of God at work, and I have seen it happen over and over again: Spiritual reality, through Christ, in the lives of people who will never be the same again because they met him!

The housewife burdened down with the load of raising a family after the father deserts them; the young coed bewildered by the crosscurrents on a large college campus and seeking roots and direction; the businessman looking for something beyond the rat race of the corporate routine and cocktail parties—all find a new life beginning when Christ is born in them. And the young people I meet in the drug scene find a lasting satisfaction that no chemical can give.

Frustrated was putting it mildly.

It was one thing for the sheriff's office in San Jose, California, to know Frank was dealing drugs to his high-school buddies regularly and heavily. It was quite another thing for them to catch him and have proof that would stand up in court.

They wanted to catch this seventeen-year-old high-school junior, and badly. The officers figured he was selling three hundred dollars a week in grass, acid, speed, and reds around his campus, and perhaps double that at week-end rock concerts.

Like many other pushers, this young man wasn't a good advertisement for his products. He had started out, like most, smoking marijuana as a freshman in high school because of curiosity and peer-group pressure. It didn't take long for Frank to lose interest in studies, sports, and activities—again, all too typical. He soon found that the older fellows who supplied the grass just "happened to have" the heavier drugs which he went on to use. Before long his hair was over his shoulders and unkempt, his school grades and conduct were a mess, his home relations soured completely, and his mind was thoroughly disorganized. The kids called him "mush-brain" because he couldn't speak or reason coherently. About the one thing he could do was deal drugs, and at that he worked hard.

He was usually pretty careful about who he sold to, but as the business grew, he got careless and the narcotics officers had their break. He sold two kilos, four pounds of marijuana, to an undercover agent and was arrested.

Juvenile hall was a jolt to Frank. The door of his unit was firmly locked, and all Frank could do as he recovered his senses was think—about what the courts would do when they learned how extensive his operation was and about his own future. Frank was not the least bit impressed by other boys in the hall bragging about their number of arrests and the institutions they had been in. He could have outbragged most of them, but unlike many of them, he wanted no part of reform schools and jails.

Wanting to change is one thing. Knowing how to go about it and then convincing somebody else you mean it is something else again.

I was introduced to Frank by his probation officer. He

was preparing the case for court but was deeply concerned about the future of this young pusher. Frank and I had some good talks in juvenile hall . . . about his life . . . about changing . . . about an inner need that all the artificial substitutes and chemical cop-outs in the world couldn't meet . . . about a God who loved him and wanted to give him a new life through his Son, Jesus Christ. One day Frank opened his life to the Lord, and it was the start of a new life that was to have an impact on the young people of two continents!

The courts don't deal kindly with pushers, even those who indicate they've learned their lesson. Laws and public outrage won't let them. But the judge who heard Frank's case was also a man of deep compassion and insight, unafraid to make an unusual ruling if it was within his power to do so and it could be justified. Frank convinced that judge to let him go home—a break he really didn't deserve but one he was ready to use properly.

His old friends were amazed to see him on the streets, but they recovered their composure enough to offer him more drugs. His consistent refusals completely baffled them.

Frank returned to school the next semester, earned grades of B and above, and was elected student body president. He served as a student teacher in a junior high school and went to the youth institution the court had considered sending him to before—only now as a worker with our Campus Life team, telling the young fellows about the Lord.

As time passed, Frank spoke to thousands of young people in high schools about drugs from the view of one who knew by experience what they could do. And he never hesitated to tell of his personal faith when asked how he had managed to get off drugs. In addition, he assisted the juvenile court and the officers who had arrested him in group meetings for teenagers who had been involved with drugs.

Then came a unique opportunity. The Brazilian schools asked us to send a drug expert to speak to the American students in their country who were getting more and more involved with drugs. Originally they wanted a doctor or adult expert, but what they got was Frank, a student who could relate to his own age group and most certainly knew his topic! The trip was a great success and has been repeated with other teenage ex-drug users.

When Frank's story was told in *High on the Campus*, a book on the drug scene I wrote with Haskell Bowen and Art Linkletter, Mr. Linkletter invited him to share his story with the vast audience on coast-to-coast television. Frank's testimony reached into millions of homes and was such a success that he was brought back a month later for a second appearance.

Frank is now enrolled in college and has worked with our Campus Life staff and on the staff of a county school drug education program. But perhaps the greatest thing of all happened to Frank recently. He and his older brother, a young man home on leave from the navy, were out in the hills hiking and talking. Tom had watched Frank through all the drug days and then had seen the change which had taken place in his life.

"Frank, I've been looking for something to really give my life the meaning and purpose you've found. Tell me about it." Frank did, and up in the hills the two brothers became brothers in Christ.

Yes, Frank is still pushing, all right . . . the greatest thing going . . . faith in the Lord.

# Chapter 3

## *This Guy Talks Like He'll Live Forever*

COURAGE CAN BE found in unusual places. And there is nothing like the confidence that comes to a person from a deep sense of God's love in his life. In fact, in an age of easy compromise and declining standards, his strength will be often a far greater influence for good than mere platitudes, threat of dire consequences, or moral exhortations. The strength a man finds within himself through the Lord can meet, and often overcome, some insurmountable odds.

The San Jose city council had debated long and hard over an issue with definite moral implications—the easing of regulations governing displays of pornographic literature at a business center directly across the street from a junior high school. Freedom of expression and interference with legitimate business had been argued by the proponents, but those opposed had argued that the place in question catered to a youth trade and therefore should be restricted. The anxious council members, fearing voter retaliation no matter which way they decided, were ready to refer the matter to the voters and let the majority rule.

A young housewife, who had sat anxiously but quietly through the debate, turned to the council and said, "Gentlemen, issues of right and wrong are not decided by a majority vote, they are decided by men with courage. A million-vote majority for something that is wrong does not make it right!"

We often hear of political leaders influenced by lobbyists, pressure groups, and campaign contributions. We may even assume all of them are controlled in this way, but this is not always so.

A political leader friend of mine stood up to the pressure interests who had tried to control him once he was in office. It wasn't easy. In doing so, he had antagonized some of his close associates and allies and had thoroughly angered some of the wealthiest and most powerful interests in the state. But he had stood firm, and I remember him saying, "I've been told if I don't give these people what they want, they'll blacken my name and get me out of office. And they may have both the money and the influence to make good on that threat. But each morning when I look in the mirror to shave or sit at breakfast with my children I have to ask myself, 'What kind of a man and father am I?' And I know what my decision has to be. I would rather be at peace with myself than have a great political career." And he did lose the next election, but he gained something far more important.

Young people have often shown me some unusual courage.

Jeanne was one of the most vivacious, attractive young

ladies I've ever known. And she was a dedicated Christian. I first knew her as an active Campus Life Club member in her high school, where she was also a good student and a popular cheerleader. After school, she often came down to help out as a volunteer worker at our office, and we got to know each other well while working on mailings, running mimeograph, and so on. I assumed that she came from a Christian home and had encouragement in her faith, but this was not so.

Jeanne's parents were both alcoholics, fighting constantly, unfaithful to each other, continually threatening divorce, mocking her faith, and generally making life miserable. Her older brother was a junkie, a drug pusher, and was in and out of jail. I probably would never have known any of this if Jeanne hadn't talked with me hesitatingly one day about the welfare of her younger brother and sister. She had managed to keep them clothed and fed from her own earned money, and it was up to her to get them up in the morning, feed them breakfast, and send them off to school on time while the parents were sleeping out another hangover. But soon Jeanne would be leaving to go away to a Christian college, and she was concerned for the future of the younger children.

The details told in a calm uncomplaining way from this charming young lady unnerved me like few experiences in my life ever had. I asked her how she kept so happy and why so few people knew of her problem. "The Lord just means so much to me, I get by," she said through her tears—tears not of self-pity but of concern for those younger children. I took her to a child protection agency and an investigation was launched, but Jeanne was a young person whose courage I can never forget.

Roger is another one . . .

"Roger, we're going to perform a biopsy—examine a piece of tissue from that bruise on your leg under a microscope. Then we'll know what to do."

"You'll tell me the results right away, won't you?"

"We won't need to. When you come out from under the anesthetic, reach down and feel for your leg. If it's there, well and good. If not, then there was malignant cancer and hopefully, by amputating, we will have gotten it all."

When Roger Garcia regained consciousness following the surgery, he reached down under the covers. His leg was gone.

His first reaction was panic and anger. He tossed and turned and had to be restrained, but the disappointment he felt was gradually overcome by the belief that he had been cured from something that could have killed him.

He didn't brood long. Five days after coming out of surgery, he was back at school! Two big problems were on his mind: he knew he would not be able to dive or enter the cross-country again, but could he wrestle? (It was his favorite sport.) And how would the girls react to a boy with one leg?

There wasn't much to worry about on either count. He was thoroughly accepted by the student body at his high school, especially by the girls. And no one could find a regulation requiring a wrestler to have two legs. As soon as his condition permitted, Rog was back wrestling with his old team—against some pretty startled opponents—and going right on with his past winning streak, too.

Even though he felt fine, the doctor at the Stanford University Medical Center kept a careful check on Roger's condition. And at the start of his junior year, the x-rays showed signs of malignancy in one of his lungs. They called him back in for another operation.

Lung operations can be among the most miserable of surgeries. When Roger regained consciousness, there were "all sorts of tubes around the room and all of them ending in me." They were needed for feeding, breathing, and waste elimination. To keep phlegm from gathering in his throat and chest and perhaps causing pneumonia, it was necessary for Roger to cough up the fluids.

"I never knew coughing could be such a difficult, painful process. The slightest cough sent stabs of pain through my whole body, and those tubes didn't help in the least.

"There were times I was afraid I was going to die, and other times I was afraid I wouldn't! More than once I was ready to give up, then I'd try to rest, and when I woke up, hoping all this was a bad dream, I was still there and so were the tubes."

Roger improved steadily, and so did his spirits. He got to know a number of the other patients—including many young cancer patients. More than once he would go to the room of a friend only to find the bed empty and freshly made—the disease had claimed another victim. (Cancer is second only to traffic accidents as the leading cause of death among young people.)

Inquiries about his condition didn't bother him, but having to talk about lung cancer did. "That's a terrible thing to have," Rog commented. "I don't even smoke!"

Later there was more lung surgery—mercifully less complicated and less painful than the first lung operation. During that first operation he had lost twelve pounds, but he lost only one pound during the second one. He also learned to cough by himself the second time around, and didn't miss that needle in his throat one bit. And he startled the nurses by asking for some food a few hours after surgery. "We hadn't counted on this so soon," they countered when he asked for a menu.

"Look, after all I've been through here you wouldn't want me to die of starvation, would you?" Rog insisted. They compromised on some liquids.

Many school groups heard about Rog, and he never hesitated to answer queries about his physical condition or the faith that sustained him through all his ordeal.

"I know I couldn't have gone through this on my own. If it had been up to me, I would have either driven off the Golden Gate Bridge in my Chevy or taken a good stiff dose of those pain pills and ended it.

"But when I was thirteen I opened my life to the Lord and invited him to become my Friend and Guide. I want my life to count for him. That's why I'm active with Campus Life and teach a Sunday school class at my church.

"Some of my friends were praying that God would heal me. I've never asked for that. I've said, 'God, if this is what you want, I'm willing to go through it so you'll be honored. Just give me the strength.' And he has, along with so many opportunities to tell people what he means to me and can mean to them."

Some of his friends are more upset about his illness than Roger is. One asked, "Why does a nice guy like this have to go through such misery when so many kids throw their lives away?" It's not an easy question to answer.

Later, Roger—tall, handsome, blond, muscular—was

the picture of outward good health. A plastic leg seemed to function like a normal one. But there was a new problem—an inoperable cancer of the spine. Linear accelerator and x-ray treatments were used to slow this latest growth. As a result, Roger's back was nearly all scar tissue.

Rog kept up with his school work, and following the second lung operation, he finally quit wrestling, but he still helped coach the team and kept the records. He recovered sufficiently to return to school.

The prognosis? Roger always answered in his usual straightforward manner, "Medically, my condition is terminal. There is nothing more the doctors can do. They say I will die."

Before Roger passed away, he spent a lot of his time speaking to other kids at various high schools, Campus Life clubs, and at the county juvenile hall and rehabilitation ranch.

To see this eager, handsome, young man confront a youthful audience with the fact of his condition sobered the most casual teenager, but Roger continued, "There is no need to be morbid. Am I really very different from you? Aren't we all terminal cases—bound to die? Who is to say anybody here will live longer than I? Face it, we're all just one heartbeat away from eternity. None of us can choose when or how we will die, but we can choose what we will die for. The important thing is to be ready . . . to live a full life for God . . . to know the Lord . . . and know where we're going when this life is over. And believe me, I know!"

When he finished his talk with the boys at the county

ranch, they asked some questions, including some on wrestling techniques. Roger answered by going over to a mat and pinning a couple of guys in a demonstration.

One startled fellow commented as Roger was leaving, "That guy talks like he's going to live forever!"

That's right. He will.

# Chapter 4

## *Traveling to Nowhere*

JOHN DOESN'T LOOK like your standard young doper. His ears are uncovered by hair, he smiles a lot, and adults like his politeness.

Most adults, that is. There are some fairly smart police officers up and down the West Coast where he has roamed since his parents divorced seven years ago. The police and John know each other pretty well.

"Believe me, the last place for an American kid to get in trouble is in a Mexican border town like Tijuana," John advises. He and two buddies skipped school once and headed there in a jeep. Before long, the trio was picked up as suspects after a robbery-stabbing incident in a bar.

The officers spoke little English; the youths spoke little Spanish. But the officers were quite sure they understood the meaning of John's friend's long hair. "They really roughed him up, shoving and slapping him after he was handcuffed. I was pretty sick inside, thinking my turn might be next."

All three were taken to the Tijuana jail. "It's filthy . . . hot . . . overcrowded," John recalls. "All the things you take for granted if you're in trouble in the U.S. —notification of your parents, an attorney, your rights, halfway decent food—they just don't exist in a border jail. We were just a mile or so from the American border, but we might as well have been on the other side of the moon."

The police questioned them, but got few answers. They then hinted at the possibilities of bribery, but the boys had no money. Two days later they were turned loose anyway—to find their jeep in the police parking lot stripped of its radio, spare tire, and extra battery.

Being the victim instead of the burglar was a strange twist for John, who had seen the inside of American juvenile halls eight times before he was seventeen. Probation—and breaking it—got to be a routine as John was involved in thefts and drugs until finally he was sent to a county juvenile rehabilitation facility.

A combination of good facilities, dedicated staff, and excellent program often succeed in straightening out the twisted values of many of the young wards; not so with John. He viewed the ranch largely as another game to play, another system to beat. He made a satisfactory initial adjustment and eventually worked his way up to a job that gave him access during the day to most parts of the ranch.

That position became most opportune when a couple of buddies managed to smuggle in a small quantity of carefully hidden drugs after a home visit. John was able to arrange for their distribution.

If the ranch program was not succeeding too well in

really reaching John, neither was our Campus Life staff. When other boys who had turned their lives over to Jesus Christ approached him on the subject, he brushed them away.

Distributing drugs had its problems, however, mainly the fear of being caught once again. John quit his drug involvement about the time the ranch staff began investigating. Fearing he would be implicated, he decided, with two others, to run away.

"Taking off from the ranch is no great accomplishment," he says, "with no bars or fences, no locked doors. The big obstacle was a creek. A few days before, it had been a shallow stream; on this day it was deep and plenty cold. It was slippery walking, and I was almost ready to turn back and forget the whole thing."

So were the other two, but no one would suggest it. "So we had to keep on going. We stayed in a field alongside the highway, ducking every time a car came by. Finally we got to a main intersection with a service station.

"I looked a mess, but I went inside anyway to try to talk the attendant out of a dime. I don't think he could decide whether I was a filthy hippie or a stupid hunter. Anyway, he gave me a dime, and I called a friend to come pick us up."

Damp and discouraged, they spent three hours along the road nervously dodging police cars before the ride came. "The whole thing was boring and sickening by that time," John remembers, "but we were in so far we couldn't go back."

It was decidedly the wrong day to escape. Near the home of the two other escapees, a gas station attendant had been shot and killed. The three boys had nothing to do with it, but the police were looking for them as prime suspects for awhile. The heat so unnerved John's friends that they decided to turn themselves in. That left John on his own.

There was only one thing to do—hit the road again. A few weeks later he was back again, looking for an old friend named Terry, who might help him stay out of sight. Terry had already been to the state youth authority and knew his way around. Not only was he a savvy guy, he would have access to some false identification.

John found him, but he had no ID available. Instead, Terry was excited about a new kind of life he said he recently discovered with Jesus Christ. Memories of the guys at the ranch flashed through John's mind . . . but this time he listened. Terry talked about what he was going to do with his life, now that he had quit drugs, and told John he needed to make the same switch.

Terry took him to see Chris, another friend who had recently lined up with Jesus. This *really* blew John's mind. He remembered the night Chris was so stoned on acid he had attacked somebody on the street and then sent two policemen to the hospital before being subdued. Chris had been sent to the same ranch, but he wanted the help the ranch staff offered and had also made a commitment to the Lord. He told John about his most recent trip to the ranch—to talk about Jesus as a new member of the Campus Life drug abuse team!

"Well, what do you think I ought to do?" John asked Terry when they were alone.

"All right man, this is going to be tough . . . but I'd say two things. Accept Jesus Christ. And return to the ranch."

"No way!" John replied, "I'm never going back there."

He later asked Chris the same question. Amazingly, he got the same two answers.

In his quiet moments, John fought with himself. He didn't want to be "religious." He was clever enough to make it by himself. Or was he? After all, the police were looking for him around the clock. What about Terry and Chris? Why hadn't they turned him in? Evidently, they weren't just trying to prove something; they were honestly wanting to help him with his basic problem.

He finally decided they were right. John made the same decision that had changed his two best friends—he invited Christ into his life.

Meanwhile, the word was spreading among John's other friends that he was off the ranch. Some of them planned a celebration party, and a few evenings later they began to gather in a home. The party wasn't exactly a public event, but the word had been spread to the right people, and it was sort of like old times for the guys and girls who hadn't seen each other in a while.

In the dimly lit room, the sweet, acrid smell of marijuana hung in the room as the joints were passed from hand to hand. The bennies and the reds were all in stock that night, waiting to attack John's new commitment. The main thread of friendship between these kids was drugs, and so the conversation ranged from recent busts to tales of good highs as they waited for the guest of honor.

All the elements of his life up to now were there waiting for him—booze, dope, illicit sex. John walked in, was greeted, sat down. But he wasn't happy. The kids joked about the police not being able to find them, and he smiled weakly.

Finally, he stood up and began moving toward the door.

"I just don't belong here," he said quietly, to no one in particular. Some kids didn't hear him, others couldn't figure out what he meant, but by then he was outside and gone. He had walked out of not just a party, but a pattern of living that had been a bummer and was now strangely altered.

The word got to John that I wanted to see him because I said so over my radio program, naming him! I finally found him on a holiday at his mother's. That night I met with John and he introduced me to Terry. Together we talked about John's new life and the responsibility he had to face if people were to believe in his sincerity. He knew what I meant. He had to turn himself in. That was almost as difficult as the first decision. But John knew it was the only right thing to do.

The next day I went with him and his father to juvenile hall where he surrendered. A few weeks later he told a juvenile court judge why. "I've proved to myself I can stay away from drugs even when they're all around me. I'd like to work out some plans to aid guys in the same problems I've had, so when they come back to the community they can handle the temptations, the old crowd, getting readjusted to school.

"I've found the most wonderful thing you can imagine. God's love does make a difference. I'm really anxious to share it."

John is no longer in an institution. He's a student in vocational school and has produced my "Speak Out" student talk radio show. He's active in church. After six downhill years, he's headed in a new direction.

Her beautiful eyes flashed with hate. There were no

tears, and I had the uneasy feeling she had long since cried all she could. What made matters worse, as I vainly groped for some word of consolation or encouragement, was the simple fact she had good reason to feel the way she did. We both knew it.

Marilyn was a lovely girl, and it was easy to detect a natural radiance longing for expression that all her pent-up bitterness could not quite hide. She was keen, alert, and intelligent.

I first met her at a church youth conference where I was speaking. She was sixteen, and we had several long talks between the various sessions. Marilyn had never had much church involvement. In fact, she had come to the conference only because some friends at school had invited her with promises of a good time. Once she arrived, she entered into all the activities and seemed to enjoy them. It was only when she talked about her own life that the happy smile gave way to the deep hostility that was just below the surface.

Marilyn's parents had rejected her. She hadn't lived with them since she was a very small child. And she had been passed back and forth to stepparents, relatives, and foster homes.

Her current foster home was number seven in three years. It was neither better nor worse than most of the others. "You know why those people keep me?" she asked. Not waiting for a reply, she went on to answer her own question, "It's for the money. That's all. They make good money with several foster children, and then they gripe about every dime they have to spend on us."

"I happen to know all foster parents aren't like that," I countered.

"The ones I've had are!" she replied emphatically.

If her adult experiences had not been pleasant, what about her relationship with her peers? "The boys at my school don't care for girls as people. They're out for sex. You know, take a girl out for an evening in a nice car, spend some money on her, and then take what they want." And she gave them what they wanted—then added the guilt and hate she felt afterwards to what was already an overflowing supply of both.

Her point in talking to me was primarily to dispute my messages on God's love. "That may be good talk for these suckers who have good homes and lots of friends, but I know better," she said.

"Many of these kids have problems at home too. But don't you feel they are sincere in their beliefs? And the adults who work with them are people who genuinely care for them."

That much she would concede. These were good people, in fact, so good she was afraid she just might be letting her emotional guard down only to have them disappoint her again and drive her further back into her shell.

One of our most capable girl counselors, who had known Marilyn, came in on the discussion and added a deeply meaningful note to it.

"Marilyn, if nobody else cares what happens to you, I do."

Marilyn laughed, "I've heard that line before. What possible difference could it make to you what happens to me? Just wait till I do something you don't like, and that will be the end of that." Marilyn knew how often friendships turned out to be disastrous, but she had finally met her match in a counselor who did care and was not about to be deterred by language or actions designed to drive her away. And here was something Marilyn couldn't handle by putting in a neat little compartment labeled "rejected," namely, a Christian who cared.

I was so concerned for Marilyn and her needs that I carefully followed up on what happened after that week at the conference grounds.

She found some real friendships in the church group and finally decided that if people were willing to accept her she would have to accept herself. Then she could begin to accept other people. Several months later she experienced the deep love that comes from an experience with Christ. And she grew in that love and faith, helped along by her new-found friends. She developed poise, confidence, and abilities and went on to complete her education and get a very responsible position in a large department store. Marilyn had an active and full social life and became engaged to be married to a fine Christian airman.

It was several years later when Marilyn and I met again. This time I was impressed not only by her beauty, but by her poise and charm. We talked about her plans for the future and her enthusiasm for life. Then we both had to leave for a very important appointment. It was her wedding day.

I performed the ceremony. Yes, they did live happily ever after. It wasn't a storybook life with all happy endings. But there were genuine strengths to face every family problem. And now she and her husband have two children who are fortunate enough to have a mother and father who know how important their love is to each other and their children.

"Look, Chuck," the officer told Charles Alexander, assistant superintendent of the James Boys Ranch, "I've got a boy on my hands I want you to take."

Usually when the ranch was asked to take a boy it was with the thought they could help him through their counseling, education, and work programs. And while, as a county institution near San Jose, California, they had to take whomever the court sent, obviously their interest centered on boys they could help.

"The truth is I don't think you can really do much for this kid, but we've got to do something with him. We can't send him home. His own family members are deeply into drugs, and the whole neighborhood he lives in is one mess of addicts and pushers."

"What about the boy himself? What has been his involvement?" Mr. Alexander asked. "You name it; he's used it," was the reply.

"Even heroin?"

"Yes, he's been on the stuff for quite awhile. He steals to buy it and then sells it as well. For a boy sixteen years old, he's been around. He's hard-core drugs."

Kids on heroin don't produce many success stories. Nine out of ten either die from an overdose in some cheap skid row dive or end up with long terms in a prison somewhere. Manuel, a young Mexican-American, seemed headed down the same road. At best, it was felt that the ranch would only delay the inevitable.

Chuck Alexander has worked with delinquent youth too long to be a starry-eyed dreamer. He is above all a realist, but he's a black man who came up the hard way himself, cares for kids, and doesn't leave his Christian concern at home when he comes to work.

After further conversation, Chuck agreed to ask the

ranch committee to accept Manuel. This was all the officer wanted or expected, but Chuck had far more in mind. If he was going to accept the boy, it was to do everything possible to help him.

There was plenty going against him. He was a heroin user, lived in a neighborhood known for drug use, his own family was involved, and at this point not one Mexican-American youth from Manuel's area had successfully made it after release. Manuel certainly didn't look like a good risk to change that sad pattern.

But the boy had some things going for him. He was intelligent, well built, and even the use of drugs had not quite destroyed what had once been the makings of a fine athlete. Furthermore, Manuel was very likable. But most important, he really wanted to quit drugs; he was long past the point of admitting there was any real satisfaction at the end of a needle. Being arrested had given him one chance to kick the habit, and he knew it. That was all there was to go on. It was interesting, but not all that promising.

Coming to the ranch was not an easy adjustment for Manuel. First he had withdrawals, and then he had to get used to the ordered routine of ranch life and schooling— not an easy assignment for a boy whose life up until then was divided between stealing and getting loaded. But he got off to a good start, probably because of a careful balance between the patience of the staff and his own persistence.

Chuck introduced us; Manuel told me his story. It was easy to like him. I heard him out and then asked if I might share with him what I had found to give my life the strength and purpose he seemed to be looking for.

Manuel was willing to listen to, but not necessarily accept, what I told him about the Lord. He knew a great deal about religion and even some things about the Bible, but that God loved him and could change his life was an absolutely new and compelling thought to him. That he would have to consider. He would have to arrive at his own decision and in his own time.

He was doing well in his studies, gained valuable insights from his counseling group, and made the ranch wrestling team. Also, Manuel was faithful in his search for spiritual answers, spending considerable time talking with our drug abuse team fellows who had met the Lord and been delivered from drugs. He was an avid questioner in our Bible discussion groups and was diligent in reading his *Living New Testament*.

The decision had to be all his. One night when I arrived at the ranch, Manuel was waiting for me. "Mr. McLean, I want you to know I've accepted the Lord into my life, and it's the most wonderful thing I've ever done."

The commitment gave him added strength, determination, and new direction. This was more than a substitute for drugs, but Someone to believe in, work for, and challenge his potential in every area of living. He rapidly became one of the most dedicated and respected young men at the ranch. And he shared his experiences in several meetings in the community as well as in the Gospel Films production based on our drug abuse book, *High on the Campus*.

Adults and young people were very concerned about the use of heroin; here was a young man who could and would relate his experience from firsthand knowledge. Heroin addiction may win over most of its young victims, but here's one young man it lost too. And if Manuel can find an answer, so can other young addicts.

A release plan was worked out so he could get a fresh start in the community while still keeping close to his family, finish his education, and stay in contact with Campus Life.

*Memo to the officer who asked the ranch to take Manuel off his hands: He's doing far better than you expected or even he bargained for. It's been rough on the outside. Real rough. But he wants to make it. If you want to know why, ask him.*

# Chapter 5
## Love Goes to Church

THE LOCAL CHURCH is important. Even its critics flatter it with attention. It has been examined, criticized, battered, and blamed for all of the world's ills. It has been called unresponsive, indifferent, irrelevant, and lazy.

Who are these detractors? Often they are those who in frustration and bitterness have left the institutional church for what they feel are more meaningful avenues of communication and service through social political action. Have they been successful in remaking the world? Hardly.

*Is* the church to blame for all our moral and spiritual ills? No. Does it have shortcomings that need honest examination and correction? Yes.

To blame the church for the moral and spiritual indifference in our society is like blaming a hospital for illness or a school for ignorance. These agencies are doing something about those problems. Talk about improving churches and suggest constructive changes, and you will find a great deal of interest and response from many

Christians. Write the contemporary church off, and it is you, not it, that becomes irrelevant.

I am a churchman. All my life has been spent in the service of my Lord through his church. And I suspect I know its weaknesses far better than most outsiders who choose to enumerate them for me.

A church to me is a group of believers doing the work of Jesus Christ. It is made up of people who have had a personal encounter with the Son of God. It is a group of people serving God, and it is also a local fellowship of believers meeting together, formally organized or in casual context, but gathering in his name. It is this last group that gets the attention when people discuss the church. And it is to this group that much of the criticism is directed.

Before I analyze some of these criticisms, let me admit my prejudice: I am for these local congregations. These people, of many denominational backgrounds, have been my warm friends; I have preached in their pulpits, spoken at their conferences, and met with their teenagers. Their love, prayers, and support have been the human instruments to make possible my ministry. I am grateful to them and concerned for them.

I am concerned because so many people today are indifferent to the established church and its program. Not opposed, mind you, but just going through some of the most exciting and important years of their lives feeling the church has little to offer them in the way of friendship, inspiration, and challenge. To these people, church is not important enough to oppose; it just doesn't matter that much.

Yet one would make a grievous mistake to assume that

people today are not interested in spiritual questions. There has probably never been a greater interest in the supernatural. The drug culture, mysticism, and the increased interest in astrology all indicate a desperate search for significance and meaning in life beyond routine and the material.

Many people *are* asking the right questions: Where have I come from? Why am I here? What is my purpose in life? Why is there so much strife and hatred in the world? What comes after death? These are good questions, crying out to be answered. The problem is either that we in the church have no answers or that our answers are not getting through.

But why? God's Word *does* point the way out of spiritual emptiness, and those who change or compromise the message, or substitute human philosophies in its place in the hope of being accepted as more relevant, end up as the most irrelevant of all. A person who should know the message of the Lord, but who can't or won't proclaim it, is more quickly cast aside than a secular philosopher. Most people prefer a foreign coin to a counterfeit.

Turned loose, the gospel message takes hold of men. It is like a magnet either attracting or repelling but leaving no man the same who encounters it. And a man who has genuinely met Jesus Christ will value no other experience or treasure or honor greater.

If our message is adequate, then the fault must lie in the method we have chosen to communicate it. We seem to have made the vehicle an end in itself, not merely a means of getting people to the Savior. We have constructed large religious machines and then worked feverishly and jealously to maintain them. Our success has been measured by the growing number of new members—all properly briefed, baptized, blessed, and counted—but not necessarily born again. The budget is raided to support ever-growing programs, and the success of a pastor is measured on much the same basis as that of a sales manager. The church has often been just as guilty as the secular world in using people to keep the machinery operating. This may make them strong church members, but it does not necessarily build strong Christians. Things were meant to be used; people were meant to be loved. Much of our trouble comes when we reverse the two.

I watched as one church school, in a serious attendance contest with another, debated whether a pregnant mother could be counted as two people. The decision, by the way, was that if the fifth month had been reached, the count would be two.

People who find themselves treated all week long as another number on somebody's computer card feel dehumanized when the same practice is carried over to the day of worship.

The emphasis on numbers has often produced a large, anemic organization better equipped for a vacation than a spiritual battle. I belong to a Rotary Club, and many of my associates are members of Kiwanis, Lions, Optimist, or Exchange clubs. Most of these groups require regular and faithful participation of their members. Members are required to make up for missed meetings, and a careful process is followed for the selection of new members. Size is far less important than quality. Should a good church require less? A club can set its own membership requirements. Church membership requirements are set forth in the New Testament.

Our style of worship has often not changed in years. Many of my friends who view formal, ritualistic services with some disdain have developed an informal routine, all their own, and equally firmly set. Further, the best one can hope for is that the hymn book won't be more than twenty years out of date. And that is not a plea to discard all the older songs, but rather a request to include many of the fine, newer ones. If young people are to be served in large numbers, guitars will have to be as acceptable as organs and pianos.

In most services more time needs to be devoted to worship. Between promotional announcements, offerings, and even good sermons, how much time is set aside for genuine, spirit-led prayer and worship?

Worship services are often geared to the wrong people. People are encouraged to bring sinners to the sanctuary for the pastor to evangelize. But what the unchurched sinner hears often sounds like a foreign language. And he can hardly be expected to assert such avowals as "Christ for me," "He lives within my heart," and "He walks with me and he talks with me," when nothing of the sort has ever occurred in his life.

Pastoral evangelism in and through the worship service is of dubious spiritual authority at best; the pastor is to be the shepherd of the flock, and the people are the sheep. Shepherds don't reproduce sheep; other sheep do. The church should be more like a filling station where saints are filled up, tuned up, and sent out to witness through church fellowships, campus Christian clubs, businessmen's fellowships, neighborhood home gatherings, and so on.

Christian testimony time can be a rich and rewarding experience in sharing, or it can be a trivial stringing together of meaningless clichés. The unchurched sinner would surely need a glossary to understand the following classic statement: "I want to thank the Lord for picking me up from the miry clay and setting my feet on the Solid Rock. And though I've failed him many times, he's never failed me yet, and I want to go all the way with him."

One might well argue that this type of evangelism has successfully reached many for the Lord. Of course, it has. But perhaps it proves most that God is so anxious to reach people that he will do so in spite of us.

Faithfulness is often measured by how many church meetings a person attends. "Be in the church every time the door opens" is considered the greatest service, but are there not times when the greatest service may be out on the campus, with friends, or at a secular event? Meetings can be one of the best excuses for *not* serving the Lord, a glorious device to preclude involvement with people on a personal level, especially non-Christians. The gospel is meeting—meeting with Christ in conversation, in growing experiences. Let us not be guilty of reducing that meeting to meetings.

Another criticism leveled at the local congregation is that we spend an overwhelming amount of time in committees—studying, passing motions, and preparing great reports. One weary pastor said to me as he went to meet with yet another committee when he longed to have time to be available to people, "Have you ever thought that God loved this world so much that he did *not* send a committee? He found one Man to do the greatest job in history and turned him loose to do it. Would that not be a good pattern to emulate?"

We see half-hearted, under-financed, overloaded activities passed off as a youth program. Somehow we fail to see our own young people as one of the greatest missionary challenges the church faces. A potential youth director should be selected because he can identify with young people and their problems, not because his academic credentials conform to an expected pattern.

Young people deserve the best a congregation has to offer. When interesting activities, discussions, and programs are made available, when the resources of community programs, such as Youth for Christ/Campus Life, are made a vital part of the church program, young people will have opportunity to realize the potential they have to offer in service to Christ and his church.

Church schools can come alive when the tools of contemporary secular education are applied. Visual aids, multi-media presentations, relevant subjects taught by competent, interested, and capable teachers, choice of courses, and team teaching can all be used to good advantage. Stimulating courses like "Reading Tomorrow's Headlines Today" (Prophecy), "The New Morality—Who Says Right and Wrong?" "Contemporary Issues," "Dating, Marriage, and Family Life for a Christian," "Science and/or Faith," etc. can all be offered with students signing up for them just as they would at high school or college.

It remains one of the great shames of our day that the most racially segregated hour of the week is on Sunday morning. The military, hospitals, and schools either have been or are being integrated. To some extent business is integrated. Only labor unions rank alongside churches in their resistance to change. When the racial mixture of a community changes, the white church often flees to the comforts of the suburbs. And somehow the gospel message that is supposed to recognize neither Jew nor Gentile, bond or free, is very much color conscious. If there is one place in the world where you would expect a man to be color blind, it's where he kneels to pray; but not so.

And then there is that all-important matter of money. So much is needed, yet so little is going outside the channels controlled by the church. One pastor said to me, "I am never afraid of money going out of my church to those works I believe in that are represented to my people. The more they give outside, the more they will give to our local work."

No one has a right to dictate to a Christian where he should invest the money the Lord has entrusted to him. Yet I have never understood why a man who, in the course of his daily business life, thinks big, can turn and be so small and petty when it comes to the work of Christ. I would expect him to support his church, but to make him feel guilty when he chooses to give some support elsewhere to those works in which he believes or that have spiritually helped him or his family is a crude and unnecessary invasion of his Christian freedom.

Many churches, including some of the largest, will expose their people to the finest of speakers and ministries and then all but refuse to let their people participate in the ministry that has been such a blessing. Then they wonder why their people are lethargic and not growing. They need to be a part of the ministry with their prayers and gifts—*impression without expression leads to depression.*

Dr. Oswald J. Smith, the great Canadian missionary statesman and pastor, was once asked if he feared having his congregation give too much money . . . would it not kill the church? Dr. Smith replied if it did kill the church, which he doubted since his work was prospering in so many ways, he would stand over the ruins and rubble and declare, "Blessed are those that died in the will of the Lord."

What can a church be? It can be warm, open, friendly to people of all ages and all backgrounds. It can rejoice when God blesses the church up the street of another denomination just as much as when it is blessed. It can reject the motto, "We've always done it this way," and change methods (not message, please) when new methods show promise of being effective.

It can recognize that the church is not merely a building and a schedule of services, but people demonstrating their faith in love, concern, and involvement on the campus, in the neighborhood, and at the factory. The church can be a training ground, a prayer center, and a source of encouragement and financial help for interchurch ministries in the community. It can say "we care" with compassion, funds, and personnel to the underprivileged, the disaster-ridden, the physically and mentally ill, the delinquent, the imprisoned, the ghetto dweller, the aged, and the lonely, whether they are across the street or around the world.

The church can say to the young, "We want you, we welcome you. We accept you, we're willing to listen to your views, no matter how radical, and we ask you to listen to ours; we'll care for you more than we'll worry about your style of clothes, the length of your hair, or the beat of your music."

The church can encourage its members to be active participants in the community and in government and not allow leadership to go by default to the selfish and un-principled. It can see that the facilities are used as often as possible for every conceivable form of outreach to make people feel at home when they come to God's house.

And are churches doing these things? Yes, they are. And if their sincere, dedicated service to Christ doesn't make headlines down here, it does in Heaven.

The church is dead? People who say that haven't been around lately. A few are dead, some are sick, but many of them are getting better. Perfect? Hardly. But wanting to improve? Yes.

Many are coming out of exile from their self-imposed ghettos. The breath of fresh air in spiritual awakening and renewal is wonderful to feel. And it is happening. Church people are God's people and mine. He loves them. So do I.

# Chapter 6

## *Love Learns Patience*

STEVE WAS A REBEL. If you met him, you wouldn't suspect it. And if you checked out his background, you wouldn't expect it.

To start with, Steve was from what could be considered an ideal home. He loved his parents, and he admits that his parents were deeply interested in him and the other children, gave him a good amount of independence and trust, and always had time for him. The family enjoyed a good standard of living.

Further, he was raised in a good church where his dad served on the board. The church itself is an active, aggressive one with a full range of activities for young people of all ages. And Steve was in on those activities as far back as he can remember. He accepted Christ in his early teenage years, the expected thing from a boy with such an upbringing, and he followed his public decision by being more active in the youth groups and in the teen choir. It would be logical to conclude that here was a fine boy of whom the church and his family could well be proud.

But in his junior year in high school Steve got interested in the happenings around campus and began to take notice of the crowd that took their thrills and kicks in things that had always been off-limits to him. Being around this crowd soon led him to believe he was missing something. Booze was pretty good, but marijuana was better. He had to be talked into smoking it the first time, and he had to admit it wasn't really much of a sensation, but at least now he was doing what the swinging crowd did. He was in. No more just going to church and playing the good-boy role. It was time, he felt, to see what all these things he had been warned against were *really* like. He found out, and at quite a cost.

"Nobody I knew stayed with just grass," Steve explained. "When there's other stuff available—pills, tabs, even the needle—a guy is going to try it and pretty soon keep using it."

The drugs, the fast crowd, and the late hours didn't help Steve's grades in school. He just barely passed his senior year to graduate. His parents were concerned, of course, and often talked to him about it, but he couldn't bring himself to admit to his parents what he was really doing. When his dad asked him point blank if he used marijuana, he angrily denied ever having done so. By now, lying came easy.

Things went from bad to impossible after graduation. He couldn't go on to college; he wouldn't hold a job. Whenever he was home, he spent most of the time in his room with his records and psychedelic lights. Incense covered up the sweet, acrid smell of marijuana.

He quit going to church. His appearance was unkempt, his hair overly long, and his ambition zero. He was either home in his room or out in his van with his doper friends.

It is hard to describe the heartbreak that his parents went through. They sought the best counsel available only to be told that nothing could be changed until the boy wanted to change. They worried, and they prayed. Most important, they never gave up.

"I wanted my folks to get really mad at me and order me out of the house," Steve said. "Then I could go out with my crowd and tell them my folks had thrown me out and have a good excuse for hating them and rejecting everything they stood for.

"We had some tense arguments. They felt I was hurting my younger brother and sister, and I was sure several times it was all over. They would tell me they hated everything I was doing to destroy myself but that they still loved me and this was my home. No matter what I did, they came back with patience and concern. It almost blew my mind!"

Steve started selling drugs to get his own supply, which is the reason most young pushers operate. But then several of his buddies showed him a faster way to greater financial reward—burglary. The system worked well. They'd check out a house to be sure no one was home, then roll Steve's van into the driveway, break in, and empty the home of anything and everything of value.

Now Steve could move out of his own home, tell his parents he was working, and have all the money he needed for drugs. It was an exciting but dangerous life, doomed to failure.

Steve knew he was wrong. No matter how hard he tried,

he couldn't get his family and church training out of his mind.

"God never left me," Steve comments. "But he did make me miserable. I had pushed him off the throne of my life and was running everything myself. But he was always there knocking; the battle going on inside me was unbelievable. Sometimes in my more lucid moments, I would even talk to the other guys about God and how wrong what we were doing was. But they'd just laugh because a few minutes later I'd be just as stoned as they were."

A guy named Gary joined the group. He had been in several juvenile institutions but finally had been given a good opportunity to stay in the home of a fine Christian family. But Gary didn't make the adjustment to that style of living, so he left. He got with Steve and his companions and suggested they rob the house he had just left the day before—lots of nice clothes, some rare glassware, some of the latest albums belonging to the young man of the house, Dan Poley, and, last, but not least, Dan's two drum sets.

That last item cinched the deal. Steve really wanted a drum set, so the job was planned.

The next day after school let out, I, by chance, met Dan at his house. As we walked into the opened front door, we couldn't believe what we saw. The place was turned upside down, everything of value was gone, and Dan's room was completely bare. It was a shattering experience for the family; among other things lost were mementos from Dan's father's twenty-two years of Air Force duty around the world. Later Dan sat down to write a list for the police of what was taken and thought to himself, "I'm a pretty lucky guy to have all these things." Then he remembered; he didn't have all those things anymore. They were gone.

Three days later Gary was captured after a wild chase through a shopping center in which Dan and I joined with the police. The arrest almost produced a riot, seven police units were needed to calm the belligerent crowd, but finally the suspect was whisked away.

Dan and I saw Gary later that evening at the police station. We talked about the tragedy that had been part of his life since Gary had first left home at age thirteen.

"You guys helped catch me, and I understand that, but, now I want you to do one thing for me. If they capture Steve, I want you to get to know him and help him all you can. He's a really great guy, and he'll be ready to listen to what you have to say."

Since that was a rather unusual request to come from a handcuffed young burglar in a police station, I took serious note of it and agreed to help Steve, when and if I ever met him.

"You can find him," Gary advised. "He thinks a lot of his folks and with Thanksgiving coming up in a few days, he'll stop by and see them. You tell him I sent you!"

It wasn't quite that simple. I did phone Steve's father and went over to visit the family. They knew some of the problems, but the whole story was a sad revelation. They agreed to cooperate.

The next day they called to say that Steve would indeed be home for the holiday dinner and I could meet him if I came over right after the evening meal. But they couldn't guarantee he wouldn't bolt from a stranger or predict what his reaction might be.

"When my parents answered the door and let this stranger in, I didn't know what to do," says Steve, describing the events of that night. "My first thought was that he must be a nark. But when I found out it was Gordon McLean, I remembered hearing about him from church, his radio show, and from some of the kids. He shook hands and asked if the two of us could talk in my room.

"We went up there and sat down. I knew what he wanted to talk about, but I was amazed at how much he knew. There wasn't much for me to say as we frankly turned my life inside out in a blunt conversation. The only question was: What was I going to do about it? Keep on going downhill or do an about face?

"The decision was mine to make, and Gordon sat silently while I tried to clear my mind. Finally I looked over at him and said, 'Will you pray with me?'

"Gordon doesn't need a second invitation when a guy says that; he just starts praying. And then I prayed and really poured out to the Lord all that was tearing me apart inside.

"We went out and talked with my folks, who couldn't believe that all their prayers, love, and patience had at last paid off. They had their son back, but perhaps not for long. I made an appointment the next day with the police to spell out what had happened. There was a lot to straighten out. Sergeant Phelan, a San Jose policeman, met with me. He was firm, every inch a cop. He wanted the truth and all of it. But he was fair, and he said he'd meet me halfway. He later did far more than that.

"I was charged with burglary and had to appear in superior court. I had a fine Christian attorney, James Gifford. I pleaded guilty, several other charges were dropped, and I was to return for sentencing after the probation department prepared a report.

"Judge McInerny leaves you no doubt you've been to court when you come before him. Before my turn for sentencing came, I watched several young fellows get long jail terms and one man was sent to state prison. Then it was my turn.

"The judge pointed out that the deputy district attorney was urging a jail sentence but that the police officer had put in a request for leniency because of my cooperation. So I was going home, with a suspended sentence and a fine."

Steve is free now, working regularly and continuing his education. A motorcycle accident laid him up for awhile, but he's recovered.

As well as keeping up with his studies, Steve is active in his church and helps in Campus Life high-school clubs. He's a valuable member of our drug abuse team, speaking to teen and parent groups, and is featured in our film on the drug scene, *High on the Campus*.

Steve is what he is today—thanks to the help of many people, including a police officer, an attorney, a judge, and even a kid who was his partner in crime. But in human terms he owes much to his parents who never gave up, loved him, prayed for him, and who eventually saw their young rebel surrender to a new Master.

"Throughout our long ordeal there were some assurances in God's Word that sustained us," relates Steve's father. "One of these is 'Teach a child to choose the right path, and when he is older he will remain upon it' (Prov. 22:6, LB). He may stray when he is younger, but if his home and his teaching have been what they should be, that influence will not be in vain. I hope Steve's experience can be an encouragement to other families going through similar heartbreak and battles."

# Chapter 7
## *Trying on Jesus*

HE SHOULD HAVE done well—he had expressed great interest in our Christian fellowship, came regularly to the meetings, talked a good deal about what he had read in the Bible, and seemed to be striving to live up to what he was learning.

But he failed. Despite a public profession of faith in the Lord and involvement in many church activities, something went wrong. The old crowd at school had a strong influence; they kept telling him, "A little religion never hurt anybody, but don't get too serious about it. Besides, how can you be sure all that Bible stuff is really true?" And he went along. Doubts became the justification for an unyielded will.

Doubts are the work of the devil. Very few people believe in a devil these days, which suits him very well. He is helping circulate the news of his own death. Satan has very little trouble with those who do not believe in him; they are already on his side.

Being tempted is not a sin; giving in to temptation is the sin. Sometime I want to write an article titled "What to Do with Temptations besides Making Friends with Them."

Temptations can be met successfully. We know this is true when we read in Matthew 4 about the temptations of our Lord and how he dealt with them.

*The first temptation was to urge Christ to turn stones into bread.* Satan advocated social reform without spiritual rebirth; he suggested filling men's stomachs but not their hearts.

But Christ would not agree to be a baker instead of a Savior; he would not be a social reformer in place of a Redeemer. He rejected any plan which promised to make men richer without making them holier and quoted the Scripture, "Man shall not live by bread alone . . ."

*The second temptation was to thrill people with scientific wonders.* The devil was saying, "It's the spectacular that people want, not the divine. Relieve their monotony and stimulate their jaded spirits, but leave their guilty consciences alone!"

We repeat that temptation today when we admire the wonders of science and ignore the Creator. Man tempts God after he has destroyed our cities with violence and hate and then shrieks out, "Why does God not stop this war?" We tempt Christ by saying that he has no power unless he shows it at our call. That is exactly how Satan tempted Jesus in the desert.

Christ answered this temptation by going again to the Scriptures, "Thou shalt not tempt the Lord thy God."

*The third temptation was to make a political deal, an easy accommodation, with the prince of darkness, a co-existence between good and evil.*

Satan offered Christ the kingdoms of the world; that Satan could even make such an offer is some indication of his power. It was not God who had delivered any of the kingdoms of the world to Satan; mankind had done so, by sin. Christ could have mankind as long as he promised not to redeem it.

But Christ considered the loss of all the kingdoms of the world less than the loss of a single soul! So in answer to Satan's blasphemous request, patience gave way to anger, and Christ turned for the third time to the Word of God for his answer, "Get thee behind me, Satan."

Each time Satan tempted Christ, our Lord met the adversary with a quote from the authority of Scripture. Is there any better shield for us to wear in meeting the onslaught of an unremitting enemy?

But the devil isn't our only source of problems. Sometimes we give him too much credit. Other forces are at work even in us. The *world* in which we live tries to inculcate its value system into the life of the believer: nothing is wrong unless you're caught . . . eat, drink, and be merry for tomorrow we die . . . anything is all right if the motive is one of love . . . throw off the inhibitions of a bygone era and do your own thing . . . people are there to be used, and so on.

Paul answers this by saying: "Don't copy the behavior and customs of this world, but be a new and different person with a fresh newness in all you do and think. Then you will learn from your own experience how his ways will really satisfy you" (Rom. 12:2, LB). Get a new and different set of values from those of this sick world; get your values from God and his Word.

Another source of our problems is the desires of our

own flesh, the old lusts and appetites that keep cropping up. Paul gives some practical advice to young Timothy about this: "Run from all these evil things and work instead at what is right and good" (1 Tim. 6:11, LB).

Even in this age of loose morals and the pill, many young people learn from firsthand experience the danger of lingering in the place of temptation. The automobile, for example, has become far more than a mode of transportation to eager youth. It is a ticket to independence, a status symbol, and more to the point, for some, an escape from prying parents as well as a portable tavern and a four-wheel bedroom. Adolescents are running to, not from, dark secluded corners where lusts and temptations, like photographs, develop best. Such inadequate relationships, *Playboy* magazine aside, can hardly be called love.

Even the mass pleasures of our day—the pornographic movie, the vulgar novel, the drug culture and the music that often promotes it—bring no respite from meaningless inadequacy. Can anything be more pathetic than the organized joy of the jaded?

The Word of God says don't play with evil desires. Get out. Run as fast as you can in the opposite direction. Make some firm decisions about your personal standards and stick with them. People who wait until the time of temptation to decide what their standards are have no standards. Don't linger in the devil's playground.

But what do you do when you fall into temptation?

The Bible tells of two prominent men who fell into temptation about the same time, Judas and Peter. Judas betrayed Christ for money. Peter's problems were a little more involved. Several times Peter was tempted. Once when our Lord bid Peter to walk out on the water (Matt. 14), he did for a short distance, and then he fell and Christ had to rescue him. Why the fall? Because he worried about the winds; because he concentrated on natural difficulties; because he did not trust in the power of the Lord and failed to keep his eyes on him.

Then at the time of the crucifixion Peter denied even knowing Christ. How could that happen? First, danger lurked for Peter because of his exaggerated self-confidence in his own loyalty. A second danger was his previous failure when he was told to "watch and pray." He did not watch, for he fell asleep; he did not pray, for he substituted activism for spirituality by swinging a sword. A third danger was the physical distance he kept from Christ which might have been a symbol of the spiritual distance separating the two. Any distance from the sun of righteousness is darkness. Looking at Peter and Judas together we find there are some interesting parallels, and differences, between the two.

First, our Lord called them both devils. Second, he warned both that they would fall. Third, both denied our Lord. Fourth, our Lord tried to save both—Peter through a look and Judas by addressing him as "Friend."

Finally, both repented; Peter went out and wept bitterly; Judas repented by taking back the thirty pieces of silver and affirming the innocence of Christ on any charge of wrongdoing.

Then what makes the difference between the two men? Peter repented unto the Lord and Judas unto himself. The difference was as vast as that between a cross and a psychoanalytic couch. Judas admitted he betrayed innocent blood, but he never wished to be bathed in it. Peter knew he had sinned in denying the Lord three times and sought redemption. Judas knew he had made a mistake and sought escape; Peter knew he had sinned and sought redemption.

The tragedy of Judas is what he might have been. What if he had turned to the tree of life rather than the hanging tree?

There are those, of course, who never get as far as committed involvement with Christ as Peter did. They want to "try on Jesus for awhile" like a customer might put on a new pair of shoes in a store and walk around the sales floor for awhile testing out the comfort and glow of new leather but never buying the merchandise. They are like the spectators at a sporting event who want to cheer the winners on, carry the coach off the field after a spectacular victory, but who never join the team or suit up for the game. They will follow a leader to the point of convenience, convention, and comfort, but never sacrifice. In a world that believes in the primacy of the economic, they will not accept one who says, "Blessed are the poor . . ." or "Blessed are those who mourn . . ." Those who believe all values are relative and truth uncertain will not follow one who declares, "I am the way, the truth, and the life." A society which believes a person must resort to every manner of chicanery and duplicity to get ahead will be appalled at one who declares, "Blessed are the pure in heart." A world that emphasizes personal pleasure will find itself strangely out of step with one who says, "If anyone wants to be a follower of mine, let him deny himself . . ." These people may "try on Jesus" for awhile, but they will soon leave him alone.

There is no halfway with Christ. He is either Lord of all or not Lord at all.

In Matthew 2, there is a reference to King Herod who

was curious about Jesus and wanted to know all about him, but that is as far as it went. And Herod will forever be the model of those who make inquiries about faith but who never act rightly on the knowledge they receive. Like plane announcers in the airport, they know all the routes, but never travel. Head knowledge is worthless unless accompanied by submission of the will and right action.

Love is no halfway measure. It sent Christ to the cross. It cost Him everything. It will cost us no less.

# Chapter 8

## *The Risks of Love*

ORGANIZATION AND EFFICIENCY are good things. Too much of Christian work is haphazard; I believe firmly it is a grievous sin to be late, to bore people, to ignore correspondence, or to show any of the other trademarks of the thoughtless and indifferent. So by all means be organized if being so will give you more time for people.

Of course, you can be so busy you have no time for people. It's less risky that way. If you're open, you'll have to take chances, you'll have to risk being misunderstood, hurt, even thought of as a fool. And the people you love may not be mature enough to accept what you're offering. Like children, they may hit back, cry, reject. But still we must love because Jesus told us to.

I was hurrying down the corridor of juvenile hall to an important conference. I passed a group of the wards heading to a school class; some smiled or nodded a greeting, others paid me no attention. One young man stepped out from the group, reached to shake my hand, and said,

"Good morning, my name is Cliff." Then, embarrassed by his boldness, he quickly stepped back into line and went on his way.

It was an unusual action, and so later in the day I checked through the unit log, found a boy named Cliff listed, and sent for him. He seemed both surprised and glad to have a chance to talk.

He was a junior in high school, personable, intelligent, and in the juvenile hall for the third time because he was considered beyond family control. I learned that his eagerness to be accepted often put him at odds with the counselors and the other boys. He found friendship hard to take. If anyone was friendly to him, he either cut them off so as not to get hurt or endeavored to manipulate them for his own ends and far beyond reasonable limits. As a result he often found himself isolated from the group. When he was really anxious for attention, he attempted to slash his wrists.

I found Cliff very open to the gospel, responsive to the chapel services, and intrigued when we talked about how Christ could build an inner strength and security so he would no longer need to lean so heavily on those around him. We became rather good but mutually cautious friends.

A few weeks later I arranged to take him out of his receiving room over to the radio station for my weekly student phone-in talk show. I let him help produce the show, getting the calls ready for me on the air, and he did a very thorough job. On the way back to the hall I stopped by a friend's home to deliver a message and left Cliff in the car. When we got back to the hall, he commented, "You don't know what a chance you took to-night. When you stopped at your friend's home, you left the keys in your car so I could listen to the radio. I almost took your car. I wanted to see what it would do and visit my girl friend for a few minutes and enjoy some freedom for awhile. I was watching for a chance to take off the whole evening we were out and you really gave it to me."

"If you had the chance, why didn't you go?" I asked, realizing full well I had given him ample opportunity to do exactly that, though I hadn't given it a moment's thought at the time.

"I don't know. Maybe it's because you trusted me without even thinking about it. But it was scary for me. Man, if you're going to take me out again, wait till I let you know I'm ready to go and can handle it."

"Okay, Cliff. Will you also let me know something else? When you're really ready to risk everything you've got built up inside you, give up your games, and turn your life over to Christ?"

"Yes, I will," he responded intently.

And he has . . . on both counts.


There's another reason for noninvolvement besides wanting to avoid risk: viewing the mission of the Christian as that of merely getting people into heaven.

But suppose you read the Scriptures and see where our Lord cared about every area of a man's life—physical, mental, social, as well as spiritual. Suppose you are challenged by the miracles of our Lord in ministering to the needs of people as when he healed the sick, fed the multitudes, turned water into wine at a wedding feast, cured the lepers, and ministered to an adulterous woman who also happened to be a despised Samaritan.

When our Lord said to "render unto Caesar that which belongs to him," did he mean simply the narrow obligations of a coin for the tax collector or was he speaking of the whole area of concerned, Christian citizenship? I choose the latter.

How often have we decried the choice given us at the polls and simply picked the lesser of two evils? How easily we forget that bad men often get elected because good men won't run for public office.

And suppose we decide to tackle the problems of our polluted environment, labor unrest, campus turmoil, and racial hatred? The sound of support in these areas from the Christian community will often become a very small whisper indeed. Now I am not saying that social consciousness should replace evangelism. I am not concerned for the welfare of people in place of my Christian faith, but rather because of it.

And I suspect many of us have a long way to go in this direction. Take racial attitudes. Prejudice is so easy. "I got a good deal, but I really had to jew him down." Why not Baptist him down? or Methodist him down? Or consider the image of white as good, black as bad. On television, the bad guys wear the black hats, the good guys, white. In our churches the black heart in the church school illustration stands for sin. But the Scriptures never refer to sin as black, rather as crimson. How easy it is to shed glycerin-eyed tears at a missionary convention over the dark heathen half a world away while ignoring people of the same color in our own community.

A pastor-friend of mine was so convicted by the problem in his community that he served on the human rights commission working for open housing, more jobs for minority groups, and better schools in ghetto neighborhoods. All the while he continued a fervent evangelistic ministry, but with an increasingly unsympathetic constituency in his home church.

Many of the Christian people were ashamed and embarrassed by his activities, if not openly hostile. Church leaders made it clear that, except for a few token members, minority people were not welcome in their church. It was done, of course, under the guise of "them not feeling at home here. They'll be so much happier in a church with their own people, don't you think?" No, he didn't think so and eventually he was forced to leave his church.

Prescribed dress, political attitudes, and intellectual conformity are often required for Christian acceptance. How tragic the belief that we know what is best for other people has led to a lot more than forced short haircuts on unconvinced adolescents. It also starts wars.

# Chapter 9

## *You Can Bank on It!*

Does God who loves us want Christians to prosper? Or is there some divine virtue in being poor? Many people ask these questions; I often did.

I learned that God wants his children to prosper. Read 3 John 2, "I wish above all things that thou mayest prosper and be in health even as thy soul prospereth." Think of it. God's wish is that your body, your health, and your prosperity all succeed as well as your soul! Why then aren't there more prosperous Christians?

Mainly because many of us have guilt feelings about being successful. We feel that somehow we should sacrifice and not really enjoy the nice things of life and the material comforts that God gives us. And if we don't feel this on our own, there are those who will gladly encourage such guilt. In truth, the people who sacrifice the most inevitably say the least about it; but often others less prone to give up things are more than adequate at talking on the subject. Is it misguided dedication or envy that prompts this concern?

I remember a prominent and materially successful Christian who was once asked by a reporter, "Don't you feel you could help the cause of Christ more if you gave away all your material things to serve the Lord?"

His response was specific. "I don't think you reporters would believe in my message any more if I hitchhiked into your town than came in an airplane. I thank God for the material things I enjoy because I know they are from him. And as long as he has provided them and allows me to enjoy them, I will be grateful. If the time ever comes when I must give up every material and monetary advantage I enjoy to preach the gospel and better serve the Lord, then I will gladly do it and be thankful for the privilege."

It was a good answer. As far back in Scripture as the first psalm, the writer suggests that a man should get his advice from the right people, his pleasure from the right things, and his values from the right source. If he does, "Then whatever that man does shall prosper."

Certainly a wrong attitude keeps many Christians from prospering. They look to people, agreements, or jobs, instead of to Christ to meet their needs. Philippians 4:19 reminds us "And it is he who will supply all your needs from his riches in glory, because of what Christ Jesus has done for us" (LB).

God supplies the needs. Anything or anyone else can only be the means he chooses to accomplish it. What a tragedy to mistake the means for the source, to worship the channel instead of the Giver. But how exciting to know that behind all of God's expectations he put his power and his provision. What better security guarantee for the future does a person need?

But there's another problem. Embarrassingly, God can't trust many of his children with money. He gives them a little, allows them some success, and what happens? They spend it all on themselves. "We've got so many bills, so many things we need right now. But later on, when we've got things squared away, then we'll give to the Lord." It's a familiar story.

If God is on the list of financial priorities, he's not at the top of it, but rather somewhere down the line after all the expenses, obligations, and pleasures.

God wants "the first fruits" of a man's labors, not the leftovers. But can't that approach to giving hurt when you're hard-pressed to make ends meet and things are rough? Not really. I've never known a man who stood faithful to God in good times who went hungry for long in bad times.

This lesson was no easier for me to learn than it may be for you. In fact, I had so little confidence in my ability to really put the Lord first in the matter of my own giving that I decided to open two bank accounts—his and mine. When I received any funds, I instantly put at least 10 percent in my giving account for the Lord's work. And it hurt at times with school expenses, a car repair bill, a new suit needed. But I made my commitment and stuck with it; the Lord's money went into the Lord's work.

But a strange thing happened. I never missed that money. First, there was the real, genuine joy of giving back to the Lord a portion of that which he had given me. And second, God always gave back more to me than I gave to him; I stumbled across the amazing truth that a man can't outgive God!

Then I discovered my amazing principle wasn't very

new after all. God had put it in his Word centuries before: "For if you give, you will get! Your gift will return to you in full and overflowing measure, pressed down,
shaken together to make room for more, and running
over. Whatever measure you use to give—large or small
—will be used to measure what is given back to you" (Luke
6:38, LB).

Frankly I didn't start giving faithfully and regularly
with the thought in mind I'd gain anything back materially. Not at all. Then I found it was happening, not just
as some odd phenomenon, but as part of a very basic
scriptural principle.

I've shared the principle with many young people just
starting out earning their first pay checks and newlyweds
building a home and family together. Sometimes they are
skeptical or scared (I can certainly understand that because I was!), but God never lets down his end. Be faithful to him, even in difficult times, and he will meet your
needs . . . plus!

I have to believe God for a large budget to be met each
month for our ministry among the young people. It's no
great credit to me; I actually have no other choice. I really
don't know how to raise it all. Besides, I'm often too
busy in actual teen ministry to take time off for fund raising. I like to ask people to share financially in the work of
the Lord, though, because I know giving is one of God's
choicest ways of blessing people. Often all I can do is
trust him, and he never fails. Yes, he puts us through
testing times to enlarge our faith and remind us of our
dependence on him, but he still meets the needs.

There's another principle of Christian responsibility
that our Lord carefully made with the illustration of the

man going away who left three servants various amounts of money to increase for him. It's related in Matthew 25. When the traveler returns, he rewards the servants who multiplied their money and rebukes the one who merely held on to it.

I have repeatedly heard this parable used to illustrate the importance of faithfulness and stewardship, and those points are well made. But a very basic, overriding principle in the illustration is rarely referred to. Not only does Got expect us to be good stewards, but he expects us to multiply to the maximum that which he entrusts to us —talents, abilities, and money. Yet many people simply put their money away for a "rainy day," and the way they go about it we could well conclude they expect a monsoon more than a sprinkle.

Nothing is said here to discourage providing for one's family; that is sound. Nothing stated here should encourage foolish or reckless investments. But if the illustration of our Lord means anything, surely it means we have a serious obligation to do all in our power to make the money he has trusted us with grow to its greatest potential, so greater can be our share in giving to his work.

And God, in his love, can use financial testing to make us mature spiritually. He can also use it to bring a man to him. Bill Rose, of the *Oakland Tribune*, shared with his readers the story of one of my close friends:

Conn Bauer, a six-foot, seven-inch, 285-pound mountain of a man, had his eyes on a wrestling career when polio brought him face to face with death and the God he had ignored.

"Anyone as big, as ugly and as strong as you shouldn't mess around in this construction business but make some real money in pro wrestling," a construction firm boss had told him.

But one Saturday as he was washing his car in the 110-degree sun that beamed down on San Bernardino, Bauer became a victim of "a tremendous, blinding headache" and went to bed. Three days later he was flat on his back in a hospital fighting for his life as the result of the polio attack.

"In ten days' time these powerful hands and arms that once performed feats of strength were suddenly useless," said Bauer. "I couldn't even feed myself.

"I was a very bitter man. I couldn't understand why God had picked on me. I'd already lost the sight of my left eye in an accident as a youth. I hadn't done anything really bad.

"I was even more shaken when the doctor told me there wasn't an iron lung big enough for me and that if the polio progressed any further I was a dead man.

"The night after he told me that I really prayed for the first time in my life. I told God I'd be his man if he'd just get me out of this mess. For the next few hours I felt a warmth like being in the Father's arms, and I became convinced I'd be all right.

"Ten days later I hobbled out of the hospital with a limp and a partially paralyzed left arm that was in a brace for six months. By the use of physical therapy, life was restored to the affected parts of my body.

"During my recovery I began to realize that if I put my trust in God I could turn what I once considered a tragedy into a blessing. He showed me that the time had come to make a living with my head instead of my big strong back.

"As I looked to him, opportunities began to come my way. I had the opportunity to come to San Jose as the boss of a construction crew and put in fifteen hundred homes.

"Within months I organized my own company to do concrete work and began to make a lot of money.

"I also got a bad case of 'churchianity.' I joined the 3 and 10 Club—I went to church three times a week and gave the church a tenth of my money. I tried to recapture the feeling I had had in the hospital.

"The more I worked at it by getting involved in more of the activities of the church where we belonged, the more frustrated I became. Finally I just told the Lord that if there wasn't anything more to the Christian life than I had found I was ready to chuck the whole thing as a bunch of hokey," Bauer recalls.

About that time Bauer's wife, Clare, asked him to go with her to some evangelistic meetings in San Jose. He went reluctantly, he said, "because I didn't want to hear some leather-lunged Bible-banger try to scare me into heaven."

After he got to the meeting, he said his interest became somewhat aroused because the speaker was a businessman like himself. However, he still was not sold on what he was hearing.

"First this fellow said that God had a plan for my life. That didn't interest me too much because I had a great plan going of my own.

"I had a successful business, a $150,000 home, prestige in the community, and the finest stable of horses in California.

"Then the speaker said we were separated from God by sin. I didn't buy that completely because I knew I had done enough good things that would outweigh the bad things so that on the day of judgment I'd come out okay.

"When the speaker said that faith in Christ as Savior and Lord was the only way to be reconciled to God, and that I could have a personal relationship to him, I really listened. This was new to me.

"I knew Jesus as Savior but not as Lord. However when I learned that making Christ the Lord of my life meant I'd be working for him and thought I might lose some of my luxurious living, I balked."

Bauer said that after the second night he "canned the whole thing" but that his wife went "the whole route and asked Christ into her life. This really bugged me.

"All my life I had tried to stay clear of religious fanatics, but now I was sleeping with one. Our marriage began to fall apart. I knew I needed what she had, but I didn't want to pay the price."

Bauer related how the money market dropped out from under the construction industry and how three of the biggest homebuilders he was a subcontractor for "went belly up" owing him $250,000—$250,000 he needed to pay his bills.

Bauer said his business was doing about $1.5 million a year putting in two thousand foundations in Alameda, Contra Costa, and Santa Clara counties when this financial disaster hit.

"It looked like everything was going to cave in—that

I might lose my family, wife, and business. Finally, in desperation, I got on my knees at 4:30 one morning and told God I was ready to try his plan in that mine wasn't working out so well.

"I just asked Jesus to come in and take over with no strings attached. My life began to change. I fell in love with my wife all over again. My five kids became precious instead of a bother to me. And within six weeks I'd recovered all but fifty thousand dollars of what was owed me.

"I then realized that God didn't want to wipe me out. He just wanted me. While that experience cost me fifty thousand dollars, it was well worth it. If the Lord hadn't jolted me the way he did, I'd never have come to my senses.

"I've learned you have to be more than a professing Christian. You have to be possessed by the power of God. Life really and truly began for me at forty when I asked Christ to take over my life.

"As big as I am, I'm no match for the world or for Satan. But with Jesus Christ I have the supernatural power that makes victory possible in every situation."

# Chapter 10

## *Love Your Enemies*

OF ALL THE many warnings in the Bible, there is one I have never had to worry about. "Woe unto you, when all men shall speak well of you" (Luke 6:26).

Throughout my time in Christian service, my steps have been dogged rather persistently by an array of critics. Probably the most dangerous thing in the ministry is to fail, but I am sure the next most dangerous thing is to enjoy any measure of success or prominence. There are those who reason if you're a success in your work, you're not doing things the way they would do them, so obviously something is wrong either with you or with the particular ministry.

Critics come in several categories; those who don't know what you're doing or why, and those who know very well but disagree with either your message or your methods. The first group results from my failure to keep them informed, and I should honestly share with them my beliefs and objectives. They have the potential of becoming my best friends. With the other group, it is best to agree to disagree and go your separate ways. There is rarely much to be gained by answering a belligerent, unreasoning critic. Fortunately there is little to lose either.

I recall a ministerial-lay leadership meeting to plan a city-wide evangelistic outreach effort. Several very thorny issues had to be settled, but by far the thorniest was the proposed participation of the black churches in the community.

One pastor, his voice quivering with rage, announced, "If they come in, my church will not support the campaign!" Most of the group seemed stunned, and none were eager to antagonize the pastor of one of the largest and most influential churches in the area.

The pastor sitting beside me leaned over and quietly asked, "How much support has this brother given this effort so far?" None that I could recall.

"Then what's the loss. *People who don't help you when they're for you will never hurt you when they're against you.*" It's true, but it doesn't make the sting any less appreciated.

I first encountered opposition when I shared with an institutional chaplain in a day-long Thanksgiving program at a youth correctional facility. It was a wonderful day. We began with an early morning service attended by many of the young men, had dinner with them, later showed one of Billy Graham's fine evangelistic films, and spent the rest of the day counseling spiritually with those who desired our help. The chaplain and I were both exhausted at the end of the day but really grateful for a wonderful time of ministry.

Several weeks later a friend in the community sent me a religious paper published in the area with a front-page story headlined "Evangelical Youth Leader Sells Out to Anti-Bible Crowd." I was the youth leader mentioned, and I had "sold out" by working with a chaplain whose credentials were theologically unsound in the opinion of the paper, and further by showing a Billy Graham film. Anything to do with Graham was an anathema to this self-styled ultra-spiritual group.

I was baffled. I did not know what the church affiliation of the chaplain was until I read the story. All I knew was that he was a sincere man of God who loved the same Lord I did and was most desiring of seeing his young congregation hear the gospel. As a result, we had seen a wonderful spiritual harvest, and I left confident my chaplain friend would faithfully continue to work with the men who had responded. If heaven rejoices over one stray sinner who repents, the celestial city must have been a very happy place that day.

But all of this had no significance to my detractors. For them it was the labels that mattered. But the Scriptures disagree. "Man looks on the outward appearance, but the Lord looks on the heart" (1 Sam. 16:7, RSV). I'm on his side.

Critics in other areas can be much harder to deal with.

A married man in the service of our Lord has many problems and temptations with which to deal. So, I would like you to know, does a man who is single because, unlike our Roman Catholic friends, the Protestant religious leader is expected to be married. If he is not, the inevitable question is a suspicious why?

101

I am single but did not always plan it that way. Actually, I was deeply in love with a charming, beautiful young lady in college, and we shared many wonderful hours and experiences together. We enjoyed many common interests, including a mutual faith in the Lord.

But eventually one overriding obstacle marred that relationship. I wanted to be in an active full-time ministry, and my fiancée wanted a husband with regular office hours, a good income, and plenty of free time for her and a family. That was a choice I could not make, even to please her, and so we parted instead of announcing a long-expected engagement. It was not easy for either of us, but the decision was made. And while I have many times enjoyed the company of other women down through the years, I have never felt the same desire for marriage. In the meantime, I have been able to use the freedom my lack of family ties gives me to minister longer with more people, not, I feel, as an artificial substitute for marriage responsibilities, but as a matter of personal choice. There are, of course, many well-intentioned folk who know just the girl I should marry. One lady told me she'd pray every day for me until I realized it was God's will I marry her daughter. Have you ever been thankful for unanswered prayer?

But being unmarried is a position fraught with dangers ranging from eager friends who know just the girl I should marry to those who question my moral integrity and motives because I haven't.

I have to be cautious seeing a teenager, boy or girl, alone and even a show of sincere interest and friendship is enough to trigger dubious minds and active tongues. That some of this activity comes not from our enemies, but from within the Christian fold, makes it a bitter pill to swallow.

I have learned to be highly suspicious of the spiritual effectiveness of those who talk despairingly of another Christian; *a man who can't be trusted to tell the truth about another person can't be trusted to tell the truth about God.*

Human nature is base when it headlines and parades the real or supposed tragedies of others before their fellowmen. Some faces are never so gay as when regaling a scandal, which the generous heart would cover and the devout heart pray over. The more base and corrupt a man, the more ready he is to charge offenses to others. I have noted that vicious people like a monopoly on their vices, and when they find others with the same vices, they condemn them—with an intensity the good never feel. All one has to do to learn the faults of men is to listen to their favorite charges against others.

But it's not all on the debit side. I actually owe a good deal of thanks to my critics. They have kept me ever alert to temptations and pressures. And when I have been discouraged enough to quit the ministry, their attacks have kept me from that course. I talked one day with a close friend about just forgetting all the critics and leaving the work, and he calmly replied, "Your enemies didn't put you in the ministry. Why should you let them take you out?" That settled it.

Critics, however unkindly intentioned, have made me see my own mistakes and shortcomings and helped me improve my ministry. I certainly don't need to agree with them to learn valuable lessons from them, and I have.

Our Lord's enemies did all they could to destroy him

103

and were unsuccessful. If we stay close to him and walk in his light, they'll have an equally difficult time with us. But there's another dimension to the problem.

Learning to handle *my* attitude toward the critics was a great deal more difficult than merely deciding not to let them get me down.

You don't generally sue people in Christian circles; it isn't right and only spreads the division and scandals in the body of Christ before the whole world. And those inclined to reckless statements know of this hesitancy to call them to task and are thus able to get by with assertions that would find them facing libel or slander assertions if made in the secular world.

The Scriptures tell you to "love your enemies" and "pray for those who would despitefully use you." I found it much easier to read and quote those words before I ran into some real live enemies to whom I had to apply them.

One of my strongest critics became seriously ill. When I heard the news, I was actually happy about it and quick to comment, "He deserved it after all he's said about me." But then those Scriptures came to mind, and I knew how wrong I had been. Here was this man seriously ill, in much pain and he would be for a long time. His family couldn't help but be going through a very difficult time.

I called my staff together and said we had to pray for this man. I started by asking forgiveness for being gleeful when I first heard of his illness. The words almost gagged me, but I asked God to heal him and be with his family. I'm sure I didn't mean it that first day, but day by day as I prayed, out of duty I'm sure, I found myself meaning it more and more, replacing my anger with genuine love and concern.

The man eventually recovered, and his attitude toward me was no different. But mine was toward him, and that was the important thing.

I had learned another valuable lesson: I must act, not react to situations and people. I must set the direction of my attitude and conduct not simply as answer to what people do to me, but what I know on the basis of God's Word to be right.

And I can be thankful to my enemies for making me a better Christian and a better man.

# Chapter 11

## *Something for You . . . or for Me*

THE COUPLE MOVING into their new apartment down the street from mine were greeted very cordially by the young man and his wife who lived across the street. The new arrivals were told about schools, stores, invited over for coffee, introduced to other neighbors, and generally made to feel very welcome in their unfamiliar surroundings.

The friendly man across the street had the couple over for a barbecue, and the families went to a baseball game together. A warm friendship was developing.

One night the neighbor called and asked if he could come over and talk with the young couple for a few minutes. He was of course welcomed.

After a few pleasantries he explained he represented a leading life insurance company, a fact which he had mentioned casually in earlier conversation, and wondered if he could go over the policies the couple might have and perhaps show them some new and interesting plans.

His hosts explained they had an agent friend who had carefully and adequately taken care of their insurance needs and that they were going to continue with him and his company. But they hoped their answer wouldn't interfere with the friendship developing here.

"Oh, no, of course not. Well, I'd better be going. I'll give you a call," said the neighbor as he left.

But he didn't call, and the lady of the house noticed his wife was noticeably cooler now as well.

I've seen Christians do that, and I've learned the hard way how wrong it is.

I just couldn't get through to him. No matter what I did, Jamie didn't get the message, or pretended he didn't. His current confinement in the Santa Clara County, California, juvenile rehabilitation facility after several trips to juvenile court certainly proved his inability to manage his own life, all sixteen years of it, and he was sharp enough to know it.

If he admitted his need to himself, that was certainly as far as it went. He was not about to tell anybody else he had problems he couldn't handle—not the counselors, the other wards, nor me, one of the ministers working with the staff. Whenever he chose to discuss his problems—and such occasions were rare even though he was in regular discussion groups designed for that purpose—he chose to blame his parents' lack of understanding, a poor choice of companions, an unsympathetic dean at high school . . . anyone and everything but himself for his stealing and use of illegal drugs.

He was no trouble in the institution. In fact, he was reasonably popular with everyone; he had a pleasant enough disposition, and did well on the athletic teams. He had been at the institution long enough to learn the ropes in getting along; he was polite; and he did both his school work and detail assignments well enough.

But the counselors and I knew we weren't reaching him. He was going through the program, and in a short time would be back on the streets having done little more than just put in time, and that was *not* the goal of our program.

The psychologist told us Jamie was a manipulator, that he was a master of creating the right impression when it was to his advantage no matter what he really felt underneath . . . a real con man.

Here was a young man who needed a real change of direction, and I wanted him so much to know the Lord. I befriended him, spent a good deal of time talking with him, helped whenever I could, trying all the time to share with him how God could rebuild his life if only Jamie would give him all the pieces. But it was no use. He wouldn't budge.

Reaching him became a matter of pride with me. After all, I considered myself a pro at this business of winning people—I'd been in inter-church youth work for twenty years, and I knew all the techniques and Bible verses to use.

One day we talked about it. Jamie asked if I agreed with his counselor who had told the boy he was a manipulator, a boy who would use people for his own ends, and get what he wanted.

I agreed with the diagnosis and told Jamie so.

"Then I'm no different than you!" was his instant reply. I looked up startled and angrily retorted, "Now just what do you mean by that remark?"

"Simple. You think I play people for my own ends. That's what you do. You befriend a person, help him, get him on your side, and all the time you're after one thing— you want him to become a Christian . . . you want another convert. We'll both do what we have to in order to reach our goal. *We're playing the same game!*"

It's a good thing he had to leave then because I really didn't know what to say. But I sat and thought a long time.

At first I was angry. After all I had only tried to help Jamie. He was certainly being ungrateful. Sure, I wanted him to come to know the Lord, but wasn't that for his own good? But then came a biting question, do any of us have the right to use people . . . to be kind for a goal we have in mind . . . even though what we want is for their best interest? The answer had to be no, even if it meant shaking up the pattern of many years in the ministry —and that is exactly what it meant.

I had to rethink much of what I had learned in the way of evangelistic techniques to get on the good side of people in order to move in on them spiritually. Methods I could still use, but they must never master me or be an end in themselves. I would certainly have to leave behind counting converts, a spiritual number game far more reminiscent of scalp-hunting than it was the leading of the Holy Spirit.

I had to start loving people . . . not for what I could get out of them . . . not to win them . . . not to change them no matter how right that was or how much they needed it . . . just love them . . . period.

And it wasn't easy. When you've spent a good deal of time trying to do the work of the Spirit of God in rushing people, it takes an extra dose of grace to let him lead, prepare hearts, and open doors. I had to realize witnessing is primarily something you *are*, not something you perform or say.

But the change had its good aspects. I was more relaxed, more human, and less a religious robot. And even my congregation of delinquents responded in kind—not overnight mind you—they were much too suspicious of sudden change for that. But they became more relaxed and open. Instead of chasing them, I simply made myself available, and they came to me. Then, because the contact originated with them, they were often eager and open to what the Word of God had for them.

I never mentioned our conversation to Jamie again, and he knew me well enough to know I was initially angry. He was more interested in the long-range effect. But I continued to be friendly to him, congratulated him after a good game or when I heard he had done especially well in school or on a job.

One morning when I came to the institution, he was waiting to see me. After a relaxed visit, he got serious. "You're different now, Mr. McLean. I think you're helping more of the guys than you ever did."

"If that's true, Jamie, you deserve most of the credit. But what about you?"

"I'm not really any different, but I've been doing a lot of thinking. In a few weeks I'm going home, and I really want to make it . . . you know, not faking, but really make something of myself. Can you tell me how to do it?"

That morning I opened my Bible to show him the One who could make the difference, and Jamie opened his heart to a new life—a life, by the way, that he's beautifully continued and developed back out in the community. I'll never forget Jamie. Like many young delinquents I've known, he's made a marked impression on my life. After he taught me how important it is just to love people, then he let me introduce him to Someone who really loved him. We both benefited. It was a great exchange.

# Chapter 12

## Love on Its Knees

FOR MANY YEARS praying baffled me. It seemed really quite ridiculous to tell God things he knew already, so I often found myself asking, "Why bother?" I'm afraid my views of prayer were pretty childish. I looked on God as sort of a celestial Santa Claus waiting for my daily list of wants and leaving me very unhappy when they were not all instantly granted.

Sometimes I felt I was talking to a heavenly detective who kept minute files of all my wrongdoings to gloat over, or an ecclesiastical kill-joy waiting for me to be enjoying myself and saying, "There's one of those fellows having fun" . . . and then squish!

I know better now. Prayer is more than a speech, a list of wants and needs either real or fancied, or even a friendship. Prayer is the process of bringing my life in line with God's will. You've heard it said prayer changes things; believe me, it also changes people.

When I pray, I begin by telling God the truth. Of course,

he already knows it, but my honesty keeps any barriers from building up that would mar the relationship.

A married couple may both know the mistakes one of them made, but the problem is usually very difficult to clear up until the matter is out in the open, frankly discussed, and perhaps an apology made. In the same way I need to keep the channels to God unclogged. God isn't in need of that kind of cleansing in our relationship together, but I am.

Then I can talk with God about the responsibilities he has given me. And in this I can be very frank, asking him for wisdom, necessary open doors, material provision, strength, and additional help. He's promised these things, and if I'm in his will, then what I'm doing is his work, not mine. In that case I have every right to expect his power and provision as needed.

Further I have learned God never gives a man a job without first making that man into the person suited for the job and properly equipped. One day when our Lord was on earth, he called Simon Peter and his brother, Andrew, "Follow me, and I will make you fishers of men" (Matt. 4:19, RSV). He first made them something, then he gave them a job to do.

When I am praying I can thank God for the daily material and spiritual blessings we all often take for granted. One of my most sincere prayer times of thanks to the Lord followed a visit to a hospital for the mentally retarded. When I returned home, I was overwhelmingly grateful for faculties that were normal.

And I can commit specific situations to God saying, "Do whatever is necessary in my life to meet that need." This doesn't mean move other people; it means get me in line with his will to solve a particular problem. Change my attitude, put me where I should be, give me courage and wisdom. This is God at work through prayer.

I've learned a number of things that can keep prayers from being answered: Simply not asking (James 4:2), asking amiss out of my own selfishness (James 4:3), and not really expecting an answer (James 1:6) are among the more common reasons prayer is not heard.

A prayer may not be answered today or tomorrow, but for a sincere believer, it will be answered. It may not be answered in the way we want; it's difficult to accept no as an answer or even wait, but I've learned long ago that God knows what is right for my life and circumstances. Many times I've had to apologize to him for my impatience when I later saw his will working out for the best.

Sometimes praying is the only thing we can do. There are some people and situations that humanly nothing can be done to change. And the results of prayer in these can be amazing.

Take my friend Lennie. I doubt if he cared or even knew a group of students were praying for him. And I'm sure they became very discouraged as Len got deeper and deeper into his problems. But "the earnest prayer of a righteous man has great power and wonderful results" (James 5:16, LB). Prayer changes people. Len's friends found out how true that is; so did he.

Len's initials are L.S.D., and that gets you thinking about acid, tabs, and trips. He started high school without thinking much about drugs. Their use wasn't that prevalent at the time, and besides he didn't need or want them. He was an eager, personable young man with a lot going for him—a nice home in a good neighborhood, a better than average family income, a lot of activities and lots of friends to enjoy them with.

But sometimes good things can go faster than they come, and a guy who lives on externals can come up pretty poor indeed, even at age fifteen. Lennie's world collapsed in a heap the night the family got word his dad and uncle both had been arrested on numerous felony counts alleging fraudulent business transactions. There was nothing secret about it. The headlines not only told the story, but kept telling it throughout the trial and during the time both men went to prison.

A shattered Len was left as the man of the house, a position he was uniquely unqualified for. At best he was none too stable, at worst he and his younger brother ran loose, late, and free . . . for awhile.

"Misery loves company," Lennie comments, looking back on the situation. "And I was miserable. I quickly found acceptance in a group just as mixed up and unhappy as I was—the dope crowd at my school. We were made for each other, and we decided grass was made for us."

But Lennie discovered that grass wouldn't solve all his problems, in fact, his experience proved that it created even more problems. "Grass robs you of your ambition, your goals . . . you don't care how you look or act," Len answers. "But that's not all. If there's a greater chemical high available, you're going to go on it in nearly every instance. And it *is* available. The guys dealing grass just happen to have acid, speed, reds (seconal tablets), all the rest. That's the route I went, and so did all the crowd I hung with."

Where does the supply come from?

"Kids deal to each other. A guy scores [buys] a supply and shares it with his buddies. He usually makes enough to finance his own supply and maybe some extra. If you're involved with drugs long, you end up dealing. I did, and became one of the biggest pushers in my area as a senior in high school."

Lennie grooved on acid. He also used speed (methedrine) and dropped reds. The result? A messed up mind, infectious hepatitis from dirty needles, and expulsion from high school one month before graduation.

That might have been enough to discourage some people, but Lennie was by now thoroughly dependent on his pills, tabs, and hits. He really couldn't quit if he wanted to, and he didn't want to. Besides, he wouldn't have the foggiest idea of where to start if he were to quit, so that settled that.

Eventually a big dealer gets greedy and loose in his transactions and the police catch up. Lennie's first bust came following a high-speed chase in what the police suspected was a stolen car. Four patrol cars converged on him and his partner and for their efforts were rewarded with a glove compartment full of dangerous and restricted drugs. Lennie went to jail.

He was soon released without bail on his word to appear for trial. He needed money to pay for his attorney, so he scored some more drugs and set up to deal out of his mother's home figuring she would ignore his actions. He figured wrong, and that was Lennie's second bust in almost as many days. Once again he was released and was again arrested! Finally while he was leaving municipal court, he was arrested for a fourth time on an indictment handed down by the grand jury charging illegal sales of drugs.

Lennie agreed to save the county time and expense by pleading guilty to several charges, and they returned the favor by dropping the other counts. And then Lennie went to the county jail farm.

Jails, incidentally, are not usually good places to get off drugs, especially the one Len was locked up in with men coming and going every day on a work furlough program. One thing did help: the chapel services where another whole way of life, free of drugs, was presented. They did get Lennie thinking.

When he was released, he went looking for more drugs but stopped before he got very far. His mind was at last unclogged long enough for him to see where he was going and what he was doing to himself. It was not a pretty picture.

He decided to look up some friends who were out of the drug scene and stopped by their house. He walked in right at the time they were praying for him and for a chance to share their faith in the Lord with him.

To say they were glad to see him is an understatement. They promptly invited him to a high-school conference being sponsored by their church. Lennie couldn't really say no, so he went. "I enjoyed it. These kids had lots of fun and some good discussions. They talked about a practical faith that made sense. I was really thinking."

Shortly after, the same group took Len to hear Nicky Cruz, the former New York gang leader. Nicky minces no words in his clear-cut call to Christ, and Len was the second person to the front to give his hand to the speaker and his heart to the Lord.

From there, Lennie got actively involved in the Campus Life high-school club program and joined the drug abuse team conducting programs for students, teachers, parents, churches, and civic groups. That, plus his work, keeps him busy.

But does it make a difference?

"Yes, it does," Len comments. "For the first time in my life I feel clean, happy, relieved inside. I'm off drugs because I don't need them. I found something so much more real and lasting when I opened the door of my life to Christ. And I did that because some Christian kids cared enough to be my friend, pray for me, and help me meet their Friend. I really dig this life. Christ is where it's at."

And some friends, who believe God answers prayer, helped Len find him.

# Chapter 13

## Where Do I Go from Here?

HAVE YOU EVER listened in awe as some great servant of the Lord shared certain spiritual high points from his life and then began to feel that something must be missing from your own experience?

This lack of drama bothered me a great deal for a long time. In fact it gave me a spiritual inferiority complex until I realized that God will not fit into any man's mold—he reserves the right to deal with each of us individually. Actually, I'm convinced it is most presumptuous of anyone to say, "You've got to have the same experience we've got and in the same way or . . ." What they really mean is that unless your experience is just like theirs, you aren't one of the group or you're not as spiritual.

This tendency toward spiritual bragging is particularly true when it comes to talking with Christians about the Holy Spirit. Some well-meaning friends at a Bible conference urged me to seek the gifts of the Spirit, and for awhile I followed that urging to the point where I was so busy looking for the gifts that I forgot the giver. It also dawned on me that seeking after the Spirit of God implied that he was elusive, hard to reach, and otherwise needed to be begged for his attention. Nothing could be further from the truth. He was much more anxious to fill my life than I was to let him, and when I quit seeking and started yielding areas of my life to his control, the inflow of his power was a beautiful thing.

It is one thing for me to have the Holy Spirit and quite another for him to have me. Every Christian has the Holy Spirit, for it is he that works the miracle of salvation which the Bible calls a new birth. Tragically with many, the work of God's Spirit in their lives stops at that point.

But, as my friend John MacArthur points out, a person can take a seltzer tablet and place it in a glass of water and at that point the water has all there is of the seltzer. Not until the tin foil is removed is the seltzer free to move through the glass and take over the water. So it is with the Spirit of God. He is in our life when we receive Christ, but only as we unwrap our selfishness and yield to him, does his Spirit fully control our lives. Such an experience may come as a dramatic turning point following conversion, but it may also come much more gradually through honest introspection and yielding inch-by-inch to the control of God.

Why is this tremendous resource available to the Christian? For what purpose does the Spirit indwell our life? Romans 8 gives us some insights into the working of the Spirit in a human life. *He helps us control the lusts of our own flesh.* "Those who let themselves be controlled by their lower natures live only to please themselves, but those who follow after the Holy Spirit find themselves doing those things that please God" (Rom. 8: 5, LB).

In an age of skepticism, *he assures us of our standing as believers.* "For his Holy Spirit speaks to us deep in our hearts, and tells us that we really are God's children" (Rom. 8:16, LB).

*He helps us pray,* which is really a good thing, for how weak and inadequate our communication with God will be if done on the basis of human strength and knowledge. ". . . the Holy Spirit helps us with our daily problems and in our praying. For we don't even know what we should pray for, nor how to pray as we should; but the Holy Spirit prays for us with such feeling that it cannot be expressed in words" (Rom. 8: 26, LB).

*Our hope for eternity is from the Holy Spirit.* ". . . your spirit will live, for Christ has pardoned it" (Rom. 8:10, LB), and again, "Yet what we suffer now is nothing compared to the glory he will give us later" (Rom. 8:18, LB).

Then, most assuredly, he *guides us in the will of God.* "For all who are led by the Spirit of God are sons of God" (Rom. 8:14, LB).

And that opens up another area of spiritual concern: how can we really know what God's will is and what he wants us to do? Earlier I mentioned never receiving a dramatic call to some particular field of service and being deeply moved by hearing those who had such a calling.

Just as with the Holy Spirit, once again I was faced with the perfectly childish dilemma of supposedly playing a game of hide-and-seek with an elusive God to know what it was he wanted me to do. I spent so much time wondering about the things I probably will never know that I almost missed some of the very important things I could know just by looking into his Word!

What is God's will? For a starter, God wants us to be a child of his. ". . . he is waiting, for the good reason that He is not willing that any should perish . . ." (2 Pet. 3:9, LB). *God wants us to know his Son.*

Next, in a time of dubious values, God's standards have not changed: ". . . *God wants you to be holy and pure . . .*" (1 Thess. 4:3, LB). The age of loose conduct, gutter language, hatred between races, lying for convenience, and destroying God's handiwork in the environment around us have neither changed his standards nor lowered the wages of sin.

Further, *God wants me to have direction in my life, his direction.* "In everything you do, put God first, and he will direct you and crown your efforts with success" (Prov. 3:6, LB).

Now consider the simple statement and offer of that verse. The writer of Proverbs is not the least bit hesitant about saying that if a man puts God first, then God will direct that man's life, no if's or maybe's about it!

Now let me pose a question to you. *If* you are a child of God, *if* you are living a holy life, *if* you are filled with the Spirit, and *if* you are putting him first in everything you do, what will be the result?

What you want for your life will be what he wants! There is no other possible answer. I once saw a sign on the notice board out in front of Walnut Street Baptist Church in Louisville, Kentucky, which declared, "Love the Lord and do as you please!" The audacity of the statement bothered me for a long time until I suddenly realized it was true. If you really love the Lord, you'll want to do what pleases him; his will becomes your will and vice versa.

What a wonderful way to live! Gone is all the agony of fearing divine wrath for an unintentional misstep, the seeking after the sensational and the spectacular in religious carnivals, the pleading and begging for direction that is quietly available minute by minute to a child of God.

Dr. Bob Cook often challenges people to "live on the miracle basis." This man of God simply believes that "unless God does a miracle you're through." And he's right. But a man needs God-given confidence to live that way. He needs a mixture of sanctified sense and holy daring that will attempt the big, the unusual, or the unlovely and the unnoticed and come out on top to the glory of God.

This is real living. This is God reaching out to every one of us. This is where the love is.